CW01510797

China 2049:
The Drive for
National Rejuvenation

Tian Yingkui

FOREIGN LANGUAGES PRESS

First Edition 2020

ISBN 978-7-119-11803-1
© Foreign Languages Press Co. Ltd, Beijing, China, 2020
Published by Foreign Languages Press Co. Ltd
24 Baiwanzhuang Road, Beijing 100037, China
Distributed by China International Book Trading Corporation
35 Chegongzhuang Xilu, Beijing 100044, China
P.O. Box 399, Beijing, China

Printed in the People's Republic of China

CONTENTS

Chapter 1

Moving towards
National Rejuvenation

China's history dates back more than 5,000 years. Early in the Tang Dynasty (618-907) when there were frequent foreign exchanges, the then capital Chang'an served as a cosmopolis. From the middle of the 19th century, the impoverished and enfeebled Chinese nation was bullied and invaded by Western powers. Gradually, national rejuvenation became the Chinese people's dream for their country and their own future. They have sought to build a stronger and more prosperous country, pursuing national rejuvenation and their own happiness throughout the historical course of national liberation, state building, and social development.

The Century Dream of National Rejuvenation

In modern times – considered in China to date from the mid-19th century – China has striven to achieve national rejuvenation. There have been two stages in this process. In the first stage from 1840 to 1949, the goal was to establish the People's Republic of China (PRC) and realize national independence and revitalization and the people's liberation; in the second stage from 1949 to 2049, the goal is to promote national development, lift the country out of poverty, build a moderately prosperous society in all respects, and realize socialist modernization. In the course of achieving these two goals, the Chinese people overthrew the old world and built the PRC, making great efforts to realize national rejuvenation and build a great modern socialist country.

1. China's Record of Suffering in Modern Times – "Three Big Mountains": Imperialism, Feudalism, and Bureaucrat-Capitalism

In the course of its history, China has experienced both great successes and great setbacks, and both glory and tragedy. In ancient times, China passed through the two stages of nomadic civilization and agrarian civilization, as well as three social stages: primitive society, slave society, and feudal society. Then, China was the largest country in the world with an enormous population and advanced material culture, making a unique contribution to the creation of world civilization and the progress and development of mankind.

The appearance of Yuanmou Man whose remnants were discovered in Yunnan Province can be dated back 1.7 million years. The Chinese people mastered the techniques of copper smelting about 5,000 years ago, forging iron, manufacturing white and decorated pottery and weaving cloth about 3,000 years ago, and producing steel about 2,500 years ago. In 2070 BC, the first Chinese dynasty was established – the Xia Dynasty (2070-1600 BC). The Spring and Autumn Period (770-476 BC) saw the emergence of many word-renowned cultural figures, including Laozi, Confucius, Mencius, Zhuangzi and Sun Wu. In 221 BC, Qin Shi Huang, the First Emperor of the Qin Dynasty (221-206 BC) united China, divided the country into administrative units of prefectures and counties, and standardized the script, currency, weights and measures. The Qin Dynasty's Great Wall and terracotta warriors are famed throughout the world. During the Han Dynasty (206 BC-AD 220), when the population reached a maximum of over 65 million and the land area extended beyond 13 million sq km, the Silk Road connecting the East and West took shape – the terrestrial trade routes leading to South Asia, West Asia, Europe, and North Africa via Central Asia.

In the Tang Dynasty (618-907), there were developments in agriculture, handicraft industries and commerce, and advanced technology in textile, dyeing, ceramics, metallurgy, and shipbuilding, as well as extensive economic and cultural ties with Japan, Korea, India, Persia, the Arab countries, and Europe. During the Song (960-1279) and Yuan (1279-1368) dynasties, the four great inventions of ancient China – compass, papermaking, gunpowder, and printing spread all over the world, making a great contribution to world civilization. In the Ming Dynasty (1368-1644), Zheng He commanded seven expeditionary voyages to Southeast Asia, South Asia, West Asia, and East Africa from 1405 to 1433, creating the Maritime Silk Road and reaching as far as Somalia and Kenya on the east coast of Africa.

During the Qing Emperor Kangxi's reign (1661-1722), the population numbered over 300 million, accounting for more than one third of the world's total. Covering an area of over 11 million sq km, China was then the largest, the oldest and the most populous independent feudal state in the world. According to Maddison Historical Statistics, in 1820, China's GDP accounted for 32.9% of the world total, much bigger than that of the combined total of the then 30 Western European countries, which was 23.6%. There were 412 million Chinese and 27 million British in 1840.[1]

British historian Paul Kennedy (1945-) wrote in his book *The Rise and Fall of the Great Powers* (1987), "Of all the civilizations of premodern times, none appeared more advanced, none felt more superior, than that of China. Its considerable population, its remarkable culture, its exceedingly fertile and irrigated plains, linked by a splendid canal system since the eleventh century, and its unified, hierarchic administration run by a well-educated Confucian bureaucracy had given a coherence and sophistication to Chinese society which was the envy of foreign visitors."[2]

Following the outbreak of the First Opium War (1840-1842), a war of British aggression against China, the destruction of Chinese sovereignty and territorial integrity began, and China became a semi-colonial and semi-feudal society, plunged into the darkness of domestic turmoil and foreign aggression. Its people saw their homeland torn apart; ravaged by war they lived in poverty and despair. In 1860 during the Second Opium War (1856-1860), Yuanming Yuan (the Old Summer Palace) was pillaged and burned by British and French troops. Those buildings in Yuanming Yuan that survived or had been restored were burned for good by the forces of the Eight-nation Alliance in 1900. The Sino-French War (1883-1885) was started by the French in 1883. The Sino-Japanese War of 1894-1895 and the Chinese People's War of Resistance against

---

[1] Angus Maddison: *The World Economy: A Millennial Perspective*, Chin. ed., translated by Wu Xiaoying & Shi Faqi, Peking University Press, Beijing, 2009.
[2] Paul Kennedy: *The Rise and Fall of the Great Powers*, Chin. ed., translated by Chen Jingbiao et al., International Cultural Publishing Company, Beijing, 2006.

Japanese Aggression (1937-1945) were provoked by Japanese militarists invading China.

Since the Opium War, foreign Invaders had forced the old China to sign more than 750 unequal treaties. In 1900, the Eight-nation Alliance, or improvised troops about 18,000 strong sent by the UK, the US, Germany, France, Russia, Japan, Italy and Austria, carried out a direct invasion of China. As a result, China was compelled to sign the Treaty of 1901 requiring it to pay 450 million taels of fine silver as indemnity, the greatest such sanction in world history. Chinese President Xi Jinping said with deep regret, "When the military is backward, it is fatal to national security. I often read historical materials about modern China. The miserable scenes of as we lagged behind, leaving the country vulnerable to attacks, always cut me to the heart."[1]

During the 60 years of unequal treaties, including the Treaty of Nanking (1842), the Treaty of Tientsin (1858), the Treaty of Aigun (1858), the Convention of Peking (1860), the Treaty of Shimonoseki (1895) and the Treaty of 1901, Western powers forced China by means of war into paying indemnities of 1.3 billion taels of fine silver and ceding territory of over 1.5 million sq km. The Chinese People's War of Resistance against Japanese Aggression (1937-1945) caused more than 35 million Chinese military and civilian casualties, and over US$1 trillion of direct economic losses. The Japanese scholar Mizoguchi Yuzo (1932-2010) compared this sad situation to a giant molting python, two thousand years old, which should have been hiding in cave but was exposed to the wild, constantly attacked by beasts and riddled with gaping wounds.

---

[1] Xi Jinping: *Excerpts of Xi Jinping's Speeches on Comprehensively Deepening Reform*, Chin. ed., compiled by the Party Literature Research Center of the CPC Central Committee, Central Party Literature Press, Beijing, 2014, p. 118.

2. The Chinese Nation's Centenary Struggle for National Rejuvenation – Three Revolutionary Goals: National Revitalization, Independence, and the People's Liberation

During the period from 1840 to 1949, the invasion of Western powers, corruption of the feudal rule, and backwardness of science and technology caused China to disintegrate and plunged its people into unprecedented misery and suffering. The imperialist powers occupied the country and feudal bureaucratic forces oppressed the people, burdening them with the "three big mountains" – imperialism, feudalism, and bureaucrat-capitalism, leaving the poor and weak nation with a heavy price to pay.

To achieve rejuvenation for a nation which had endured so much, it was critical to topple the "three big mountains" and establish a new country with its people as their own masters. In order to realize national revitalization, independence and liberation, the Chinese people, unafraid of sacrifice, rose up to carry out a 100-year-long struggle.

During the Old Democratic Revolution (1840-1919), the Chinese people fought bravely against imperialism and feudalism, experiencing the Taiping Rebellion (1851-1864), the Westernization Movement (1861-1890s), the Reform Movement of 1898, and the Revolution of 1911. In 1912, the Republic of China (1912-1949) was founded, overthrowing the feudal monarchy which had ruled the country for thousands of years. With tenacity and heroism, countless dedicated patriots fought against all the odds, and sought the nation's salvation through every possible means. Despite their efforts, they were powerless to change the nature of society in old China and relieve the plight of the Chinese people.

This was a time of fierce struggle as the Chinese people resisted feudal rule and foreign aggression. It was in the midst of this struggle, in 1921, as Marxism-Leninism was integrated with the Chinese workers' movement, that the Communist Party of China (CPC) was born. The birth of the CPC fundamentally changed the China's development and course, and profoundly altered the destiny and future of the Chinese people and the Chinese nation.

At its founding, the CPC made realizing communism its highest ideal and its ultimate goal, and shouldered the historic mission of national rejuvenation. In pursuing this goal, the Party has united the Chinese people and led them through arduous struggles to epic accomplishments.

The CPC was deeply aware that, to achieve national rejuvenation, it was critical to topple the "three big mountains", and realize China's independence, the people's liberation, national reunification, and social stability. During the New Democratic Revolution (1919-1949), the Chinese people underwent the May 4th Movement (1919), the First Revolutionary Civil War (1924-1927), the Second Revolutionary Civil War (1927-1937), the War of Resistance against Japanese Aggression (1937-1945), and the Third Revolutionary Civil War (1945-1949).

The CPC united the people and led them on the right revolutionary path, using rural areas to encircle the cities and seizing state power with military force. The Chinese people completed the New Democratic Revolution through 28 years of painful struggle, and founded the PRC in 1949, thus marking China's great transition from a millennia-old feudal autocracy to a people's democracy. Following the establishment of the PRC, the CPC became the governing party and the Chinese people became the masters of their own country, joining forces in building a socialist country, and embarking on a centenary journey to achieve national rejuvenation. By any standards it was an unprecedented achievement for China, a backward agricultural country with a quarter of the world's population, limited industrialization, and few material products, to create a people's democracy on such poor and weak foundations and build a new socialist society.

The CPC was deeply aware that to achieve national rejuvenation, it was essential to establish an advanced social system adapted to China's reality. It united the people and led them in completing socialist revolution, establishing socialism as China's basic system, and advancing socialist development. This completed the broadest and most profound social transformation in the history of China. It created the fundamental political conditions and the institutional foundation for achieving all the development and progress in China today. Thus was made a great transition – The Chinese nation transformed its continuous decline of modern times into steady progress towards prosperity and strength.

3. The Chinese Nation's Centenary Development for National Rejuvenation – Three Strategic Goals: Lifting the Country Out of Poverty, Building a Moderately Prosperous Society in All Respects, and Realizing Socialist Modernization

On September 21, 1949 before the establishment of the PRC, Mao Zedong asked a question at the First Session of the Chinese People's Political Consultative Conference (CPPCC), "If our forefathers, and we also, could weather long years of extreme difficulty and defeat powerful domestic and foreign reactionaries, why can't we now, after victory, build a prosperous and flourishing country?"

History gave its answer: In 1949, the PRC was established, marking a new Long March of socialism in the endeavors to revitalize the Chinese nation. In 1979, China began to implement reform and opening up, signifying that the efforts to achieve national rejuvenation were accelerating towards socialism with Chinese characteristics. In 2012, the CPC's 18th National Congress was convened, indicating that socialism with Chinese characteristics was entering a new era and the Chinese nation could look forward to the brilliant prospect of rejuvenation.

In its 100 years of endeavors to achieve national rejuvenation, the Chinese nation has three strategic goals: lifting the country out of poverty, building a moderately prosperous society in all respects, and realizing socialist modernization. By the time China celebrates the centenary of the PRC in 2049, it will have been built into a great modern socialist country that is prosperous, strong, democratic, culturally advanced, harmonious, and beautiful. The following goals will have been met: New heights are reached in every dimension of material, political, cultural & ethical, social and ecological advancement; China has become a global leader in terms of composite national strength and international influence; common prosperity for everyone is basically achieved; the Chinese nation will become a proud and active member of the community of nations.

From 1949 to 1979: experimentation and socialist transformation. The CPC united the Chinese people and led them in completing the socialist revolution and establishing socialism as China's basic system, involving the public ownership of the means of production and the people's democratic dictatorship. This created the fundamental political conditions and the institutional foundations for achieving all development and progress in China today. Meanwhile, it was the beginning of China's winding course of exploring socialist construction. After the establishment of the basic socialist system, China faced an unprecedented challenge – the test of the century – how to build and develop socialism in the world's most populous agricultural country, with a desperately low level of productivity.

From 1979 to 2000: ensuring that people's basic needs were met and that their lives were generally decent. The CPC united the Chinese people and led them in launching the great practice of reform and opening up. This had a great impact in stimulating the people's creativity, emancipating and developing social productive forces, and energizing social development. As a result, living standards rose remarkably, and there was a significant improvement in China's composite national strength and international status. During this period, China embarked on the path of socialism with Chinese characteristics, formed the theory of socialism with Chinese characteristics, established the system of socialism with Chinese characteristics, caught up with the rest of the world, and realized a tremendous transformation in people's lives – from rising to their feet to living a better life.

From 2000 to 2020: completing the building of a moderately prosperous society in all respects. By the time the CPC celebrates its centenary in 2021, China will have finished building a moderately prosperous society in all respects and will have developed into a moderately prosperous society with a stronger economy, greater democracy, more advanced science and education, thriving culture, greater social harmony, and a better quality of life, making it possible for over 1.3 billion Chinese people to live decent lives. The Chinese nation, which in modern times endured so much for so long, will have achieved a tremendous transformation: It has risen to its feet and grown prosperous and is now becoming strong. Today, China is closer than ever before to making the goal of national rejuvenation a reality, and more confident and capable of doing so.

From 2020 to 2035: basically realizing socialist modernization. The vision is that by the end of this stage, the following goals will have been met: China's economic and technological strength has increased significantly. China is a global leader in innovation. The rights of the people to equal participation and development are adequately protected. The country, the government, and society are governed by the rule of law. All institutions have been improved. China's governance system and capacity have been modernized. Social etiquette and civility have significantly enhanced. China's cultural soft power is much stronger. Chinese culture has greater appeal. People are leading more comfortable lives, and the size of the middle-income group has grown considerably. Disparities in urban-rural development, in development between regions, and in living standards have been significantly reduced. Equitable access to basic public services is basically ensured. Solid progress has been made towards prosperity for all. A modern social governance system is in place, and society is full of vitality, harmonious, and orderly. There has been a fundamental improvement in the environment, and the basic goal of building a beautiful China has been attained.

From 2035 to 2050: developing China into a great modern socialist country that is prosperous, strong, democratic, culturally advanced, harmonious, and beautiful. By the end of this stage, the following goals will have been met: New heights have been reached in every dimension of material, political, cultural & ethical, social and ecological life. Modernization of China's governance system and capacity is complete. China has become a global leader in terms of composite national strength and international influence. Everyone enjoys common prosperity. The Chinese people enjoy happier, safer and healthier lives. China is a proud and active member of the community of nations.

The Path of Modernization towards National Rejuvenation

Socialism with Chinese characteristics is the fundamental path to the rejuvenation of the Chinese nation. The very purpose of realizing national rejuvenation is to make China a stronger and more prosperous country and allow the Chinese people to enjoy a happier life, or essentially, to build a great modern socialist country with Chinese characteristics. Socialism with Chinese characteristics has been the focus of all of the CPC's theories and practice since reform and opening up began in 1978. It is a fundamental attainment of the CPC and the Chinese people achieved through countless hardships at enormous cost.

1. Strategic Guidance for Socialist Modernization with Chinese Characteristics

Modernization is a dynamic, historical and civilized process. In the Chinese people's endeavors to achieve national rejuvenation and build China into a great modern socialist country that is prosperous, strong, democratic, culturally advanced, harmonious, and beautiful, the key is to constantly build a deeper understanding of the established rules that underlie governance by a communist party, the development of socialism, and the evolution of human society; to correctly implement strategic guidelines and projects that comply with the well-established practices of modernization; and to promote progress in China's governance system and capacity.

Comprehensively upholding Party leadership. As the vanguard of the Chinese working class, the Chinese people and the Chinese nation, the leadership of the CPC is the core in building socialism with Chinese characteristics. The key to governing China lies in the CPC. The defining feature of socialism with Chinese characteristics is the leadership of the CPC; the greatest strength of the system of socialism with Chinese characteristics is the leadership of the CPC; the Party is the highest force for political leadership. Upholding and improving Party leadership is the foundation and lifeblood of the Party and the country, which protects the interests of the people and brings them happiness.

Remaining committed to the sound development philosophy. Sound development is fundamental to national rejuvenation. China must uphold the development guideline that puts quality first and gives priority to performance. China must comprehensively implement the vision of innovative, coordinated, green, open and shared development. China must comprehensively promote economic, political, cultural, social and ecological progress. China must improve international relations, national defense and the armed forces, and the CPC's ability to govern fairly and well, striving to achieve better quality, more beneficial, fairer, more efficient, and more sustainable all-round development.

Continuing to comprehensively further reform. Only with socialism can the CPC save China; only with reform and opening up can the CPC develop China, develop socialism, and develop Marxism. Entering a new era, the CPC has united the people and led them in launching the great new revolution of reform and opening up, which is a crucial choice that shapes the future of contemporary China and a key to achieving national rejuvenation. Since the launch of reform and opening up, China's economy and society have developed quickly. Future social and economic development must also rely on reform and opening up. Reform and opening up is the most distinctive feature of contemporary China.

Ensuring every dimension of governance is law-based. Law-based governance is the basic way for the CPC to lead the people in governing the country. It is an essential requirement and important guarantee for socialism with Chinese characteristics. The core ideas of law-based governance are to coordinate social forces, balance social interests, adjust social relations, and regulate social behavior, based on the rule of law; to resolve prominent social problems in accordance with the law; to ensure that China's economic, political and social development remains both lively and orderly while undergoing profound transformation; to strengthen the rule of law in political and social activities and ensure that they are institutionalized and procedure-based.

2. Strategic Project of Socialist Modernization with Chinese Characteristics

Today, in its efforts to seek national rejuvenation, China is closer to, and more capable than ever before of making the goal of national rejuvenation a reality. To achieve national rejuvenation in 2049, priority should be given to these four aspects of modernization:

First, popular support. The biggest and most significant political issue in governance is how to win popular support. To realize national rejuvenation, it is critical for the entire Party, the whole country and the people of all ethnic groups to come together and create a mighty force.

Second, innovation. Innovation is the driving force for human development, serving as the beacon of human progress. To realize national rejuvenation, the Chinese people need to advance national innovation, social innovation, innovation by enterprises, and market innovation.

Third, institutions. Institutions provide a guarantee for human development and create conditions for human harmony. To realize national rejuvenation, the Chinese people need to modernize and innovate institutions.

Fourth, capacity in all its forms. Capacity is the key to understand and reform the world. Capacity-building is critical to modernizing the governance of China. To realize national rejuvenation, the Chinese people need to improve personal ability, organizational capability, state capacity, and the CPC's capacity. Only with greater governance capacity can the Party become more successful in governance.

The strategic project of modernizing China's governance system aims to promote sound and sustained economic growth, increase the public's contribution to and gains from development, and strengthen the national capacity for sustainable development and for quickly identifying and controlling risks.

—Promoting sound and sustained economic growth. Sustained, sound and coordinated economic growth provides a material guarantee for realizing national rejuvenation. It is of top priority to improve governance and revitalize the country. To ensure such economic growth, it is imperative to fulfill the central task of economic development, and focus on improving the quality and effect of development. China needs to pursue the strategy of innovative, coordinated, green, open and shared development, striving to make economic development more fruitful, fairer, more efficient, and more sustainable.

—Raising the level of people's contribution to and gains from development. The ultimate goals and fundamental criteria of socialist modernization are to improve the people's lives and achieve shared prosperity for everyone. The rich cannot be allowed to accumulate huge wealth while the poor live on chaff. Efforts should be made to reform income distribution, improve the people's wellbeing focusing on equitable access to basic public services, and promote ecological progress characterized by environmental protection, so as to meet the public's increasing expectations of a better material life and a better environment.

—Strengthening national capacity for sustainable development. Sustainable development is social and economic development that meets the needs of the present without compromising the needs of future generations. Basic principles of sustainable development put forward by the United Nations are: first, the principle of fairness, which refers to equality of opportunity, both vertical between generations and horizontal across a single generation; second, the principle of harmony, referring to symbiosis between humanity and nature; third, the principle of progress, meaning the process of human needs ascending from lower to higher levels. To strengthen China's capacity for sustainable development and promote social and economic development in harmony with population, resources and environment, it is important to uphold a policy of people-oriented development and a vision of making development people-centered, to pursue harmony between humanity and nature, to improve people's living standards, and to build a green mode of production and green lifestyle with technological innovation and institutional incentives.

—Enhancing national capacity for quickly identifying and controlling risks. Improving this capability is key to modernizing China's capacity for governance, directly manifesting the government's macro-regulation capacity, and meeting the basic requirement for building more effective state governance. To this end, efforts should be made to comprehensively and systematically prevent and control economic, political, cultural, social, ecological, international, national defense and governance risks; to build an effective risk prevention & control system, including risk identification & early warning mechanisms, risk prevention & defusing mechanisms, and risk management & control mechanisms.

Building a Modern, People-Centered Governance System

The people are of the greatest political significance in today's China; they are the living soul of the CPC, Marxism, and socialism with Chinese characteristics. To realize national rejuvenation and build a great modern socialist country, it is essential to stick to the principle of putting people first; to making all-out efforts to build a wealth creation and distribution system in which people contribute to and gain from development, a governance system ensuring equitable access to public services by all, and a state governance system that is fairer, more efficient, and more sustainable.

1. Building a Wealth Creation and Distribution System in which People Contribute to and Gain from Development

Economic development is the foundation of modernization, the core of which is production and distribution. In the efforts to build a people-centered modern governance system, the foundation is a system of joint contribution and sharing. China should uphold this philosophy, and build an institutional incentive system encouraging mass entrepreneurship and innovation; China should continue its commitment to a philosophy of shared distribution, and build institutional guarantees promoting common prosperity.

—Building a modern economic system that inspires people's innovation. This includes modern property rights, corporate, market, fiscal, financial, industrial, trading and regulation & control systems. The construction of a better quality modern economic system that is fairer and more equitable helps the economy and can offer opportunities to entrepreneurs, jobs to labors, protection to operators, and rewards to innovators.

—Developing a modern distribution system that ensures profits are shared by all. China should continue its commitment to a people-centered philosophy of distribution for social wealth, and uphold the policy that encourages the people to contribute to and gain from development and promotes common prosperity for everyone, so as to meet the people's increasing expectations of a better life. First, a market-based income distribution incentive system should be set up to reward those who contribute most. Second, an income redistribution system should be built, in which all participate, do their best, and are rewarded and protected. China should ensure that the market plays the decisive role in resource allocation and the government plays its role of oversight to the full. Priority should be given to balancing individual incomes, government revenues and capital gains in primary distribution of national income, and to balancing government income & expenditure, public wellbeing and infrastructure in secondary distribution. China should work to see that individual incomes grow in step with economic development, and pay rises in tandem with increases in labor productivity.

Establishing a fair and modern distribution system of enterprise employees. Based on economic development, cost of living, and industry profits, China should reform and improve the national minimum wage system, the wage-pricing system (through consultation between labor and capital), and the government tax collection & management system. According to the classification of operational and public welfare enterprises, and of competitive and monopoly enterprises, intensive efforts should be made to develop a modern income distribution system for enterprises that moves with the times, to promote fair competition in the market and enable those who work harder to earn more. The key is to properly handle the relationship between workers, entrepreneurs, and technical personnel, and build an incentive system that is market-based, technology-driven, and knowledge value-oriented. This should increase workers' incomes, allow entrepreneurs to profit from their efforts, and reward those who use knowledge to create wealth and act as vanguard.

Forming a modern equitable distribution system for government employees. Based on the premise of accelerating fair competition reform which advocates that talented personnel should be introduced, incompetent ones be dismissed, and leaders be ready to accept a higher or lower post, China should develop an equitable salary distribution system which encourages fair competition, offers more pay for more responsibility, and advances with the times and in tandem with social and economic development. China should put in place a salary distribution system for government employees in public institutions and administrative organs, a government employees' salary distribution system which grows in step with economic development and is linked up with the cost of living, and a national glory incentive reward system to call for fair competition and accountability. All of this will give decent work to civil servants and incentives to those who best fulfill their duties.

Building a modern system to guarantee rural incomes. Despite the growing value of modern industry, increasing urban wealth accumulation, and rising incomes of urban residents, agriculture, rural areas and farmers remain disadvantaged. China must put in place a support system that encourages investing in farmers to guarantee their income, as requested by the coordinated social and economic development, so as to coordinate urban and rural governance. In addition, China should work faster to develop the system that is adapted to national development with the changing times, supports agriculture, benefits farmers, and advocates more pay for more work, following the principles of urban-rural integration and food security. All of this will help farmers, operators and investors to realize higher rural incomes, and ensure national food security, agricultural development, and rural modernization.

Developing a modern system for everyone to achieve common prosperity. To establish a people-centered distribution regulation & control system and keep incomes and wealth disparities within a reasonable range, it is important to prohibit and act against illicit income, adjust excessive incomes and extravagant consumption, eliminate poverty, and improve subsistence allowances. China should implement a self-balanced wealth distribution system which covers progressive taxes on inheritance, gifts, house prices and conspicuous consumption, and a tax incentive system that is more favorable for public welfare undertakings, especially for public education and healthcare.

2. Putting in Place a Modern System to Provide Equitable Access to Public Services for All

To build a people-centered modern governance system, it is essential to ensure equitable access to basic public services. The level of development and equalization of public services directly reflects the degree of social fairness and justice. With ongoing social and economic development, especially the emergence of overcapacity, the voices calling for improved public services are getting louder, with demands for standardization, equalization, and management by the rule of law. The public's expectations of a better life are the focus of China's efforts, and dissatisfaction with social problems is the target of China's reform. China must uphold people-centered and problem-oriented reform, and continue to improve the basic livelihood guarantee system concerning thousands of households.

To achieve national rejuvenation and continue commitment to the people-centered philosophy of development, China must focus on the key word "equalization", and work harder to put in place a standardized and law-based system that ensures equitable access to basic public services and gives full expression to fairness and justice under socialism with Chinese characteristics. It is especially important to give the people better access to basic education, healthcare, housing and social security, and move faster to achieve common prosperity.

Developing a modern education system that is people-centered. China should improve standardization, equalization, and the rule of law in education, and build a modern education system that embodies social fairness and justice. The goal is to give every child, rich or poor, no matter where he or she was born, fair, equitable, standardized and law-based access to education. To this end, China must ensure equitable access to compulsory education, and eliminate the serious imbalances between rural and urban areas and between different regions in public education resources. In particular, children from poor families, and students from low-income families must be able to complete their studies in basic education, vocational schools, and colleges & universities without worries. There must be preferential and compensatory investment in public education resources in rural and backward areas, and China must eliminate the problem of unbalanced development of public education in these areas.

Establishing a modern healthcare system that is people-centered. China must promote standardization, equalization, and the rule of law in healthcare, and build a national healthcare governance system that better embodies social fairness and justice and is accessible to every citizen, rich or poor, no matter where he or she was born. China should improve the baseline security level for the Healthy China initiative, and ensure that the poor can pay their medical expenses and that no-one is driven into poverty by disease.

Putting in place a modern housing system that is people-centered. China must improve standardization, equalization, and the rule of law in housing, and develop a national housing system that embodies social fairness and justice. All low-income families should have equitable access to housing, and eliminate economic hardship and poverty caused by housing. China should ensure equitable access to housing for all urban and rural households, especially poor and low-income families with housing difficulties. China can no longer tolerate the existence of shanty towns in prosperous area, dangerous and dilapidated houses, or urban slums. A basic housing security system with national unified standard should be implemented.

Developing a people-centered modern governance system to ensure basic quality of life. China should enhance standardization, equalization, and the rule of law in the work to safeguard people's basic quality of life, and set up a national governance system that better embodies social fairness and justice to guarantee people's basic quality of life. The goal is to ensure basic quality of life of every member of society, especially low-income people in a fair, equitable, standardized and law-based manner, and to maximize the living standards of the poor and low-income people. To achieve national rejuvenation, the efforts to better guarantee people's basic quality of life should cover all urban and rural poor families. Whatever the cause or situation, the system of subsistence allowances provides survival guarantee and life support, which is the lowest civil and humanitarian protection. The government must cover all the poor families and poor people in subsistence allowances system, and rescue any who fall into the "poverty trap".

3. Developing a Fairer, More Efficient and More Sustainable State Governance System

State governance is the governance of the public and the people. It should be measured against the criteria of fairness, efficiency, and sustainability.

—Building a fairer state governance system. Fairness comes from public recognition. Therefore, the people's satisfaction is the only way to measure the fairness of social development and state governance.

First, work should be done to establish a state governance information platform that better reflects the people's identification degree. This increasingly modernized network information system can present the will, sentiments, wishes and common aspiration of the people in a timely and dynamic way, providing strong public support for modernizing China's governance system. Second, efforts should be made to develop a modern institution & policy system that can better reflect economic, political, cultural, social and ecological fairness, and set up an evaluation index system for modernization that can better reflect fairness in the people's rights and opportunities, and the process and outcome of policy implementation.

—Building a more efficient state governance system. The efficiency of state governance corresponds to the people's sense of fulfillment, which is the ultimate standard to measure and test all public services and state governance. Without the people's increasingly stronger sense of fulfillment, there is neither modernized governance, nor efficient modern state governance system.

China should develop an evaluation index system for state governance that can better reflect the people's sense of fulfillment, covering the economic, political, cultural, social, ecological and governance fields. This system should also be used to evaluate, test, adjust, improve and accelerate public governance in all respects and at all levels. Further progress should be made to enhance the efficiency of decision-making, implementation, oversight, and rewards & penalties to build more efficient public governance. The people's sense of fulfillment is the criterion for identifying, evaluating and rewarding governance effectiveness.

China should put in place an identifiable, measurable, assessable, comparable and operable assessment system for state governance which consists of multiple layers and levels, is based on social information and supported by Internet technology, and involves wide public participation. This assessment system should be used to modernize China's governance system, to conduct performance evaluation of public affairs and state governance in an all-round, multi-level, open and procedural way, through statutory channels such as the CPC's National Congress, the National People's Congress (NPC), workers' congress, villagers' congress, and residents' congress, as well as other statutory public information platforms.

—Building a more sustainable state governance system. To this end,

China must stick to the well-conceived, democratic and law-based path to ensure good governance. Chinese leaders should take full account of the long-term, fundamental and overall interests of the Chinese nation to foster new thinking on people-centered state governance. To promote fairness, efficiency and sustainability, intensified efforts should be made to put in place a modern political system in which the people have the controlling voice, a modern economic system in which the people contribute to and gain from economic development, a fair and just modern system to improve social etiquette and civility, a more advanced modern system to enhance cultural-ethical development, a greener modern system to promote ecological progress, and a stronger and more efficient modern system for the governance of the country. Only by the above mentioned efforts can China realize socialist modernization with Chinese characteristics which is of fundamental, long-lasting and comprehensive significance to its people.

Chapter 2

Economic Modernization towards National Rejuvenation

Economic development is the basis for the material development of human society, providing guarantees of family happiness, social harmony and national prosperity. To realize national rejuvenation, it is essential to promote sound and sustained economic growth and a constant improvement in the quality and effect of development, make distribution fairer, and build China into a great modern socialist country featuring justice and common prosperity for everyone. To boost economic growth, China must continue its commitment to the people-centered philosophy of development; continue reforms to develop the socialist market economy; pursue the vision of innovative, coordinated, green, open and shared development; accelerate economic development in tandem with fair distribution; propel new industrialization, urbanization, IT application, marketization, agricultural modernization, and economic globalization; and promote economic development, fair distribution and sound institutions to modernize the socialist market economy.

A Great Transition in the Chinese Economy

From the outbreak of the First Opium War in 1840 to the establishment of the PRC in 1949, China – the country with the world's largest population and economically dependent on agriculture – suffered the worst economic setbacks in its history. Before the Industrial Revolution (1760s-1840s), China was a typical populous agrarian country with a vast territory, long history, profound culture, and unique politics. The added value of its agriculture accounted for more than two-thirds of GDP and its rural population was four-fifths of the workforce. Before 1820, China's population and economic output topped the world, making up over 30% of the world's total.

With the rise of the Industrial Revolution in Europe in 1750, modern industrial civilization began. During the 130 years from 1820 to 1949, there was little economic growth in China. The average annual growth rate of GDP (in 1990 US$) was 0.04%. The Chinese economy underwent a sharp decline, its share in the world economy dropping from one-third to less than one-twentieth. China was reduced from the world's most powerful agricultural economy to a backward agricultural country.

According to a study by Angus Maddison in 1999, from 1820 to 1900, the average annual growth rate of China's GDP (in 1990 US$) was minus 0.58%, and its share of the overall world economy fell from 33% to 11%; from 1900 to 1950, the average was 0.23%, and its share of the overall world economy fell to 4.6%.[1] The mode of production and the political system were out of date, with corrupt government officials, a

---

[1] Angus Maddison: *The World Economy: A Millennial Perspective*, Chin. ed., translated by Wu Xiaoying et al, Peking University Press, Beijing, 2003.

conservative ideology and culture, and agricultural science and technology that left modern China far behind the industrialized countries. As a result, China degenerated into a semi-feudal and semi-colonial country, at the mercy of industrialized colonial empires. Only since the establishment of the PRC in 1949 has China begun to realize industrialization, urbanization, and modernization.

When the PRC was founded in 1949, China was a typical backward agricultural country steeped in poverty. The population of the Chinese mainland accounted for 25% of the world total, while China's GDP equaled only 0.8%. Its per capita GDP was US$28; its poverty-stricken population made up over 65% of the world's poor; illiterate and semi-literate people made up more than 90% of the total population. It was the CPC-led political system, with the people's participation as masters of their own country, that enabled China to begin building a modern industrialized and urbanized socialist country, and to develop modern education, technology, culture, healthcare, sports and other systems. As a result, the Chinese economy grew at an average annual rate of 6.6% (at constant prices) from 1949 to 1978. This period was the preparation and accumulation phase of economic modernization in China, during which large-scale independent industrial and economic systems were established, launching industrialization and urbanization, developing education, technology and culture, and laying important foundations for economic modernization.[1]

Since reform and opening up was implemented in 1978, China has made active efforts to integrate into the global market economy and grow its socialist market economy. Three essential elements – technological innovation, educational modernization, and institutional incentives – have experienced revolutionary growth, significantly advancing Chi-

---

[1] Wu Chengming & *Dong* Zhikai: *Economic History of the People's Republic of China*, Chin. ed., Social Sciences Academic Press, Beijing, 2010.

na's social and economic development. In 1978, the population of the Chinese mainland accounted for 22% of the world total; China's GDP made up 1.7% of the world total; its economy ranked 11th in the world in scale; and per capita GDP on the mainland was US$227. By 2010, China's economy had risen to second place in the world. In 2019, with its economy accounting for 16.4% of the world total and per capita GDP reaching US$10,276, China had entered the ranks of upper-middle-income countries. It had become the No. 1 manufacturing country and the most important foreign investor in the world. Its capacity in around 220 key agricultural and industrial products led the world. In recent years, China has contributed more than 30% of global economic growth.

From 1979 to 2020, at constant prices, China's economy grew at an average annual rate of over 9%. In 2020, China's mainland population will account for about 18% of the world total and its GDP will constitute over 18% of the world total. In terms of per capita GDP, China will meet the threshold of high-income countries as defined by the World Bank. From 1979 to 2020, economic modernization will have undergone take-off, upgrading and acceleration, and will have experienced historic transitions from speed to size, from quantity to quality, and from efficiency to effectiveness. The country has achieved a tremendous transformation: It has risen to its feet and grown prosperous, and is now becoming strong; it can look forward to the vivid prospect of rejuvenation.

Comparative Strengths of the Chinese Economy

Faced with a complex international and domestic situation as well as opportunities and challenges, the Chinese economy is transitioning to a stage of high-quality development. Internationally, the Chinese economy is still in a phase of strategic development. The trends of economic globalization and IT application are surging forward. Technological revolution, industrial transformation, the knowledge-based economy, and green industry are ready to forge ahead. The drive to sustain economic development in China faces both worldwide opportunities and global challenges. Domestically, there are still problems to be addressed caused by unbalanced and inadequate development – issues of momentum, structure, quality and returns in economic growth, the need to balance the demands of resources, the environment, ecology and the wellbeing of the people, and fiscal, financial, industrial and poverty problems.

The main trends and features of the Chinese economy include:

- the change in the pace of growth from high to medium-high;
- the shift of the growth model from a speed- and scale-based model to a quality- and effect-based one;
- structural optimization, from expanding capacity to optimizing increments; and
- a change of the driving force of development from input of production factors to technological innovation.

All these trends and features represent the logic that must be fully taken into account in ensuing sound and sustained development. They are also a necessary process of evolution to bring the Chinese economy to a more advanced stage with more optimized division of labor and a more rational structure.

According to the principles of economic modernization and development, important conditions for promoting sound and sustained development of the Chinese economy are as follows:

- world- and market-based incentive mechanisms for interests that can encourage wealth creation and sharing;

- a political system and an administrative structure that can concentrate all of society's resources and efforts on nation-building;
- an international political environment that can ensure stable major country relations and facilitate world peace and development;
- international economic and trade opportunities leading to industrial upgrading and transfer on a global scale;
- huge human capital resources that can provide hard work at a reasonable cost; and
- a modern national education system supported by the government, involving all citizens and encouraging full competition.

China has strengths to sustain its economic development: first, economic scale at national level, leading to good stability and a high resistance to risk; second, depth and breadth of development at a regional level, giving the economy a high ability to adjust and extensive room for maneuver; third, substantial household savings, leading to strong endogenous drivers of investment and growth; fourth, the government's ability to regulate the economy, leading to strong macroeconomic flexibility and a high ability to self-balance. The keys to the high-quality development of China's economy in the future are comprehensive technological innovation, a modern education system, and institutional incentives.

Based on a forecast annual growth rate between 5% and 6% (at constant prices), China's economy will lead the world again before 2035. Its per capita GDP will join the ranks of developed countries before 2050; modernization of the economic governance system and capacity will be complete; the quality and effectiveness of the economy will be among the front ranks of the world; common prosperity will be achieved; and China will be a global leader in terms of composite national strength and international influence.

According to an article published by *The Economist* in 2014, in terms of nominal GDP China will become the world's largest economy in 2026, and its economic mass will exceed US$100 trillion in 2050. Goldman Sachs' forecasts show that China's economy will grow at an average annual rate of 3.4% between 2014 and 2050, and that its economic mass will exceed US$70 trillion in 2050 in terms of GDP at current market values.

According to PricewaterhouseCoopers in 2014, the global economy will grow at an average annual rate of 3% between 2014 and 2050. China became the world's largest economy in 2014 in terms of GDP at purchasing power parity(PPP); in terms of GDP at current values, China will catch up with the US in 2028, and its GDP will surpass US$53 trillion in 2050. In 2012, American economist Robert W. Fogel (1926-2013) pointed out the main reasons for China's rapid economic growth: education, urbanization, the political system, and consumption moving up market.[1]

China's Economic Modernization Strategy

Sustained, sound and coordinated economic growth is the basis for national rejuvenation and socialist modernization, providing material guarantees for a stronger and more prosperous country and a happy people. It is the top priority in governance to see China thrive. The fundamental aims for the Chinese economy are to ensure the principal status of the people and pursue sound development; to focus on improving the quality and effectiveness of the economy; to uphold the principle of invigorating China through advancing innovation, industry and the real

---

[1] Wu Jinglian et al.: *China in the Next 30 Years*, Chin. ed., Central Compilation & Translation Press, Beijing, 2012, pp. 126-135.

economy; to devote great energy to implementing the strategies of innovation-driven development, industrial upgrading, coordinated supply & demand, and geographical distribution; to apply a new vision of development; and to develop a modernized economy, striving to achieve better quality, more efficient, fairer and more sustainable economic development.

1. Innovation-Driven Development Strategy: Building an Innovation-Driven Economic Growth Model in All Respects

The innovation-driven development strategy emphasizes the need for improvement in the quality and effectiveness of the economy. China will focus on three pillars of innovation: "who innovates?", "why innovate?", and "how to innovate?" Technological innovation and innovations in management, business model and format will be integrated with new institutional and cultural models. The growth model will be more reliant on continued accumulation of knowledge, technical progress, and better labor quality. The economy will be transformed, with better division of labor and a more rational structure.

The innovation-driven development strategy has the following goals: By 2035, China will be a global leader in innovation; there will be a fundamental change in the drivers of economic growth, with enhanced international competitiveness in innovative economic development, laying solid foundations for making China a leading economic power and achieving common prosperity for everyone. By 2050, China will be a global leader in economic innovation and a leading center for scientific research at the cutting edge of innovation, providing powerful support for building a great modern socialist country and for realizing the Chinese Dream of national rejuvenation.

All-round efforts will be devoted to implementing the innovation-driven development strategy:

- developing an innovative cultural environment and forming an ideology and understanding that advocates innovation-driven development, to give innovators image, stage, market, and a positive environment;
- creating a policy framework for innovation, removing institutional and policy barriers that hamper innovation-driven development, and building a three-level innovation system (enterprise, society, and state), so as to put in place a modern innovation system, which is based on business innovation assisted by social innovation and guided by national innovation;
- modern management of innovation focusing on innovative resource allocation, evaluation systems, and team building; and
- carrying out a national innovation project, so as to transform China from a major manufacturing country to a manufacturer of quality, from being known for China-made products to being proud of China-innovated products, and from importing global brands to developing Chinese brands.

2. Industrial Upgrading Strategy: Comprehensively Developing an Economic Growth Model of Industrial Upgrading

Industrial upgrading, or industrial modernization, is an important element of modern economic development. It includes upgrading from agriculture to industry and service sector, from labor-intensive to capital-intensive and technology-intensive industries, and from primary processing technology to deep processing and finish machining.

Back in history during the era of agricultural civilization, China was the world's largest manufacturer of hand-crafted products. According to French economic historian Paul Bairoch (1930-1999) and British economist Angus Maddison (1926-2010), with its manufacturing output accounting for about 30% of the world's total, China was the largest manufacturer of hand-crafted products up to 1830. By 1953, China's share of the world's manufacturing output had fallen to an all-time low of 2.3%, while the US represented 44.7%.

According to the United Nations Industrial Development Organization (UNIDO), China's share of the world's manufacturing output rose to 3.5% in 1980, and to 5.8% in 2000, becoming the fourth largest industrial producer after the US, Germany, and Japan. By 2009, China's share had reached 25.9%, while that of the US had declined to 16.4%; China had ended 110 years of American domination of world manufacturing. In 2010, China ranked first in 17 of the 23 categories of the International Standard Industrial Classification of All Economic Activities (ISIC). It ranked second in four categories and third in two.

To promote economic growth, it is imperative to study the evolution of industrial development in depth, keep up with global trends in industrial innovation and upgrading, fully implement a development strategy of industrial upgrading, and continue to modernize the industrial, agricultural and service sectors.

—Modernizing the industrial sector. Industrialization is the process of transforming from a traditional agricultural society to a modern industrial society. American economist Simon Kuznets (1901-1985) has pointed out that industrialization is the process of modern economic development, covering the rapid growth of population and production, significant improvements in productivity, changes in the economic structure, corresponding social changes, revolutionary progress in communications & transportation, and growth of inequality between countries.[1]

In 1978, China's GDP was RMB368 billion. Of this total, the value-

---

[1] Simon Kuznets: *Modern Economic Growth: Rate, Structure, and Spread*, Chin. ed., Beijing Institute of Economics Press, Beijing, 1999.

add of the primary, secondary and tertiary industries accounted for 27.7%, 47.7% and 24.6% respectively. These proportions indicated the underdevelopment of the country's industry. In 2019, China's GDP reached RMB99 trillion. The value-add shares of the primary, secondary and tertiary industries were now 7.1%, 39% and 53.9%, indicating that China had become a developing country with a medium level of industrialization. From 1979 to 2019, overall GDP grew at an average annual rate of 9.4%, while the average growth rates of the primary, secondary and tertiary industries were 4.4%, 10.6% and 10.4%; per capita GDP grew at an average annual rate of 8.5%. At present, China is transforming from a quantity- and scale-oriented to a quality- and effect-oriented economy in the process of industrial modernization.

In modernizing industry, it is critical to embark on a path of industrialization that integrates IT application. IT application is the fundamental method for leapfrog economic development and catching up with developed countries. By stepping up the integration of IT application and industrialization, China can make its economic growth more reliant on technological progress, a higher quality labor force, and innovative management, rather than an increase in the consumption of material resources. Major measures include:

- developing a modern environment-friendly industrial system, with a strong ability to innovate, coordinate and provide quality services;
- implementing the strategy of building China into a manufacturer of quality, and making manufacturing more high-end, more intelligent and greener so that it can deliver more quality services; and
- supporting the development of emerging industries, and advancing innovation in IT, bio-industry, intelligent sensing of spatial information, stored energy & distributed energy, high-end materials, and new energy vehicles (NEVs).

—Modernizing the agricultural sector. Agricultural modernization involves high technology, efficiency and yields in agricultural production, and intensive, well-organized and market-based agricultural management. Developed countries have the following experience in promoting agricultural modernization[1]:

- devoting serious energy to technology application in agricultural production, giving priority to industrialization, mechanization, automation and IT application, and raising agricultural productivity through modern technological advances;
- intellectual investment in farmers, and continuously improving technological awareness of agricultural workers, operators and managers;
- industrial restructuring and upgrading and constantly improving the quality of agricultural supply; and
- putting in place a national security system of fiscal and financial funds that invests in farmers and ensures food security; and
- actively growing the rural transportation service industry and creating a service environment for agricultural development.

According to the National Bureau of Statistics, the output value of China's primary industry totaled RMB102 billion in 1978 and RMB7 trillion in 2019, growing at an average annual rate of 4.4%. The total grain yield was 305 million tons in 1978 and 664 million tons in 2019, growing at an average annual rate of 1.9%. The number of people employed in the primary industry was 283 million in 1978 and 203 million in 2018, falling at an average annual rate of 0.8%. China is currently transform-

---

[1] Jin Hainian: *China's Strategies for Agricultural Modernization towards National Rejuvenation in 2049*, Chin. ed., CITIC Press, Beijing, 2016.

ing from a growth-oriented to a quality- and effect-oriented agricultural industry.

To propel agricultural modernization and ensure national food security, it is important to build industrial, production and business operation systems for modern agriculture, to improve the quality, effect and competitiveness of agriculture, and to follow a resource-conserving and environment-friendly path characterized by high efficiency in output and guaranteed product safety. China's general plan is to provide agriculture with modern material conditions, science & technology and management techniques, and a modern industrial system and vision for development, to grow agriculture by cultivating a new type of farmer, and to improve the level of agricultural modernization and agricultural labor productivity and competitiveness. China will focus on developing modern agricultural technology that is efficient, safe and eco-friendly, consolidating and improving the basic rural operation system, advancing reform of the rural land system, improving the systems for supporting and protecting agriculture, promoting sustainable agricultural development, and carrying out international cooperation in agriculture.

—Modernizing the service sector. It is an important part of China's economic modernization. China aims to develop modern service industries with high technology and high cultural content that meet the needs of modern social and economic development. The total output value of the tertiary industry was RMB90.5 billion in 1978 and RMB53.4 trillion in 2019, growing at an average annual rate of 10.4%. The number of people employed in the tertiary industry was 48.9 million in 1978 and 359 million in 2018, growing at an average annual rate of 5.1%. At present, the modernization of China's service sector is focused on quantity, scale, quality, and effect.

China will adopt the following strategic measures to modernize the service sector:

First, improve the structure of the service sector. Being market-oriented and supported by technical progress, focusing on enterprises, China will adjust and improve the structure, and improve the overall quality and international competitiveness of its service industries.

Second, expand the number of jobs in the service sector. Active efforts will be made to help expand the service areas and create new jobs for service industries.

Third, develop a modern enterprise system in the service sector, and put in place an open, transparent and uniform market access system with standardized management.

Fourth, focus on specialization in producer services, and develop the information economy. China will implement the national big data strategy, and develop a comprehensive transport system that connects domestic and international channels, covers a wide range of urban and rural areas, has fully functional hubs, and provides integrated and efficient services.

3. Supply-Demand Equilibrium Strategy: Comprehensively Building an Economic Development Pattern with Supply-Demand Equilibrium

Balanced development in aggregate supply and demand is a basic condition for achieving sound and sustained social and economic development. China's general guidelines for balanced development of supply and demand are:

- leading demand and supply innovation;
- improving the quality and efficiency of supply;
- activating and releasing effective demand;
- developing an efficient and balanced economy with positive interaction between consumption and investment, and coordinated

upgrading of demand and supply;

- fostering new drivers of growth; and
- creating new space for economic development.

Advancing quality development of the real economy. To develop a modernized economy, China must focus on the real economy, give priority to improving the quality of the supply system, and enhance the economy's strength in terms of quality. China will build itself into a manufacturer of quality and develop advanced manufacturing, promote further integration of the Internet, big data, and artificial intelligence with the real economy, and foster new growth areas and drivers in medium-high end consumption, innovation-driven development, the green and low-carbon economy, the sharing economy, modern supply chains, and human capital services.

Supporting the upgrading of traditional industries. China will transition its industries up to the medium-high end of the global value chain, and foster a number of world-class advanced manufacturing clusters. China will strengthen infrastructure networks for water conservancy, railways, highways, waterways, aviation, pipelines, power grids, information, and logistics. China will work to achieve a dynamic balance between supply and demand by improving the allocation of available resources and increasing high-quality supply. China will inspire and protect entrepreneurship, and encourage more entities to innovate and to start businesses. China will build an educated, skilled and innovative workforce, foster respect for model workers, promote quality workmanship, and see that taking pride in labor becomes a social norm and that seeking excellence is valued as a good work ethic.

Moving consumption up market. In China's transition from an economic giant to a leading economic power, moving consumption up market plays an important role. The total retail sales of consumer goods grew from RMB156 billion in 1978 to RMB3.9 trillion in 2000, and to RMB41.2 trillion in 2019 – an average annual growth rate of 15%. China will adapt to the trend of higher-quality consumption, release potential for consumption by improving the retail environment, better create and meet consumer demand through improvements and innovations in supply, and continue to enhance economic development by stimulating consumption. More energy will be devoted to increasing consumption among urban and rural residents, improving consumer expectations, tapping potential for consumption, and adjusting government consumption.

To implement the development strategy, efforts will be made in the following key areas: steadily boosting spending on big-ticket items, including homes, cars, and health & elderly care; supporting new types of consumption in information, the green economy, fashion, and quality; develop new modes of consumption, including OMO (online-merge-offline); carrying out projects to enhance the quality of consumer goods; strengthening consumer rights protection; and giving full play to the role of the consumer's association to create a reassuring and convenient consumption environment. China will actively boost the return of overseas consumption, optimize the Duty Free Store layout, and cultivate centers for international spending based around important tourist destination cities.

Implementing the development strategy of increasing investment returns. Maintaining modest investment is an important way to ensure sustained economic growth. Especially during a period of rapid industrialization, urbanization and internationalization, China should enable investment to play a crucial role in ensuring steady growth by improving the supply structure and the efficiency of investment. In its efforts to expand effective investment, China should focus on creating a fair and favorable environment for investment, encouraging private capital and corporate investment, and stimulating the energy and potential of private capital.

China will give full play to the leveraging role of government investment, and increase investment in quality public goods & services, investment in human resources & human capital, and investment that can help upgrade the supply structure, address inadequacies, coordinate urban and rural areas, and boost development. Major investment projects of overall, strategic and fundamental importance will be implemented. In terms of industrial policy, China will devote serious energy to multipolar industrial development, the transformation from labor-intensive to capital-, technology- and knowledge-intensive industries, and enhancing the national competitiveness of industries.

Problems of investment scale and structure will be addressed, and China will strike a balance between moderate investment scale and sound investment structure. China will optimize investment structure, and properly handle the proportional relationship between key, fundamental, general and advanced industries. China will cultivate a development strategy of encouraging exports of independent brands and independent intellectual property rights (IPR), and fully advance the development of trade in services.

4. Geographical Distribution Strategy: Comprehensively Building an Economic Development Pattern of Geographical Coordination

The Chinese economy is mainly spread across urban-rural, regional and international economic structures. Balanced and coordinated development of these three geographical structures is an important part of China's overall sustained economic development, and a major strategic issue in economic modernization. To grow the economy, it is critical to promote balanced geographical distribution and coordinated development of the urban and rural economies, the regional economy and the international economy, and put in place a modern economic system of geographical balance and coordinated development.

—Fully advancing the geographical distribution and coordinated development of the urban and rural economies

In 300 BC, China had a population of 30 million with an urbanization level of 14.3%. In 1200, its population had reached 71 million, and urbanization had reached 22.4%.[1] In 1949, the total population on the mainland was 542 million, of which urban and rural residents accounted for 10.6% and 89.4% respectively. Its nonagricultural population in cities was 5.1%, far lower than the world average of 29.1% in 1950. In 1978, the total population on the mainland reached 963 million, of which urban and rural residents accounted for 17.9% and 82.1% respectively. In 2019, the population on the mainland totaled 1.4 billion, of which urban and rural residents accounted for 60.6% and 39.4% respectively. From 1979 to 2019, the urban population grew at an average annual rate of 4% while the rural population decreased at an average annual rate of 0.8%. China's proportion of urban residents is expected to hit 80% in 2050.

In its endeavor to promote sound geographical distribution and coordinated development of the urban and rural economies, China will be faced with population, resources, environment, industry, transport and other problems. Priority will be given to the relationship between mega cities, big cities, medium-sized cities, small towns, and rural areas. China will implement urban-rural geographical coordination that fits its prevailing reality and respects the laws of modernization, and form a sound system of urban-rural geographical distribution.

Intensive urban-rural coordinated development. In accordance with the general requirements of intensive and efficient production space,

---

[1]　Zhao Gang & Chen Zhongyi: *History of China's Economic System*, Chin. ed., New Star Press, Beijing, 2006, pp. 332-333.

pleasant and modest living space, and clean and beautiful ecological space, China will build a sound structure of working, living and ecological spaces in urban and rural areas, develop urban-rural geographical distribution with distinctive features, and promote coordinated development of urban-rural construction, population, resources, environment, and ecology. Industry will nurture agriculture, and urban areas will support rural areas. China will improve the institutions and mechanisms of integrated urban and rural development, advance equal exchange and reasonable allocation of urban and rural elements, and equalize access to basic public services. New urbanization will put people first, cultivating middle-sized and small cities and characteristic small towns, and developing a characteristic county-level economy.

—Comprehensively advancing the geographical distribution and coordinated development of the regional economy

China covers a total area of 9.6 million sq km. The territory is vast with great regional variances. Big differences exist between east and west, and south and north in natural environment, resource endowment, culture & traditions, and economic development. In 2018, the distribution of overall population across the eastern, central, western and northeastern regions was 38.5%, 26.6%, 27.2% and 7.7%. Regional GDP accounted for 52.6%, 21.1%, 20.1% and 6.2% of the national total. The total value of regional imports and exports accounted for 81.5%, 6.5%, 8.1% and 3.9% of the national total. Regional grain output accounted for 24.3%, 31.8%, 23.6% and 20.3% of the national total. Total regional investment in fixed assets accounted for 41.9%, 25.9%, 26.5% and 4.9% of the national total.

In the implementation of a coordinated regional development strategy, China will focus on building new, effective mechanisms to ensure coordinated development of different regions, and on pursuing more coordinated, interacted and holistic regional development. First, giving full play to the role of market mechanisms; second, developing more innovative mechanisms for regional cooperation; third, improving the mechanisms for mutual aid between different regions; fourth, establishing and improving regional compensation mechanisms. China will accelerate the development of poor areas. Support will be given to resource-depleted areas for their economic transformation. China will accelerate development in the border areas, pursue coordinated land and marine development, and step up efforts to build China into a strong maritime country.

To advance the geographical distribution and coordinated development of the regional economy,

First, China should uphold the principle of national coordination, avoid fragmentation in the regional economic configuration, and prevent structural imbalances in regional development. Regional economic strategy should be configured in accordance with the principles of livability and economic growth.

Second, China should adhere to the principle of institutional fairness, and develop a new model of coordinated regional development that ensures orderly and free flows of factors of production, effective main functions, equitable access to basic public services, and resource conservation and environmental protection.

Third, China should stick to the coordinated strategy principle, improve the strategy for large-scale development of the western region, revitalize old industrial bases in the northeast, support the rise of the central region and the role of the eastern region in spearheading development, speed up the development of backward and poor areas, and foster growth poles that facilitate coordinated regional development.

Fourth, China should uphold the key breakthrough principle, focus on growth clusters that support the rise of the strategic economy, and encourage the Belt and Road Initiative and strategic regional urban clusters, including the Beijing-Tianjin-Hebei region, the Yangtze River Delta, the Pearl River Delta, and the Shenyang-Changchun-Harbin region.

—Fully advancing the geographical distribution and coordinated development of the international economy

To transform from an economic giant to a leading economic power, it is critical for China to ensure a coordinated relationship between domestic economic growth and international economic development, uphold the principle of coordinated development of domestic and international resources and markets, and promote coordinated global development of goods, resources, industrial activity, technology, personnel, culture, and other factors.

Opening up has greatly accelerated growth in China's economy and trade. From 1979 to 2018, the total value of imports and exports of goods grew at an average annual rate of 18.4%. In 2018, foreign capital utilized was US$135 billion, accounting for only 1% of China's GDP. China's per capita use of foreign capital ranked after the 100th in the world, representing 50% of the world average, 70% of the average for developing economies, and 20% of the average for advanced economies. China will significantly ease market access for foreign investors, and enhance economic internationalization and globalization.

Making further ground in opening up on all fronts. China should treat the Belt and Road Initiative as a priority, give equal emphasis to "bringing in" and "going global", follow the principle of achieving shared growth through discussion and collaboration, and increase openness and cooperation in building innovation capacity. Through these efforts, China hopes to make new ground in further opening up through links running eastward and westward, across land, and over sea. China will expand foreign trade, develop new models and new forms of trade, and turn itself into a trader of quality. China will adopt policies to liberalize and facilitate trade & investment. China will develop new ways of making outbound investments, promote international cooperation on production capacity, form globally-oriented networks of manufacturing, services, and trade, investment & financing, and build up its strengths in international economic cooperation and competition.

Introducing the development strategy of global spatial distribution. Steps will be taken to improve the distribution of opening up across regions, and in trade & investment, and create new systems and space for it. China will get actively involved in global economic governance, make domestic opening up and opening up to the outside world reinforce each other, better combine "bringing in" with "going global", and promote orderly and free flows of international and domestic factors, efficient allocation of resources, and deeper integration of markets. China will cultivate new competitive strengths in being part of and leading international economic cooperation, and achieve policy, infrastructure, trade, financial and people-to-people connectivity. Efforts will be made to sublimate strategic space for spatial distribution of the Chinese economy, and coordinate domestic and international markets and resources on a global scale.

Chapter 3

Political Modernization towards National Rejuvenation

In the endeavors to revitalize the Chinese nation, political modernization is a fundamental task – China must focus on the political goal of the people being masters of their own country; steadily advance the modernization of the people's democracy, rule of law, government, and power; better ensure that political affairs are handled with integrity, that the rule of law is enhanced, that justice is upheld in the exercise of power, and that government administration is efficient; foster a fairer, more efficient and civilized political environment; and strengthen the people's participation in the deliberation and administration of political and government affairs. This is the most important issue in China's efforts to achieve national rejuvenation.

Political Progress towards National Rejuvenation

The PRC is a socialist state under the people's democratic dictatorship led by the working class and based on the alliance of workers and peasants. All power in the PRC belongs to the people. In promoting socialist political progress, China must uphold the principle encompassing the CPC's leadership, the people's position as masters of their own country, and law-based governance. This modern political civilization is suited to China's political reality, taking shape through decades of hard work of the entire Chinese people united and led by the CPC. Party leadership is the fundamental guarantee for ensuring that the people have the controlling voice and that governance in China is law-based. The supremacy of the people is an essential feature of socialist democracy. Law-based governance is the fundamental principle for the Party to lead the people in governing the country.

Political civilization led by the CPC. The CPC comes from, represents, and enjoys the trust of the people. It gathers the collective wisdom and strength of the Party and the people to build China into a modern socialist country with Chinese characteristics. The greatest strength of the system of socialism with Chinese characteristics is the leadership of the CPC. With this strength, the Party can act in earnest to protect the people's right to run the country, pool social resources to the maximum, and improve the efficiency of state governance. According to the Constitution of the Communist Party of China (2017), "The Communist Party of China is the vanguard of the Chinese working class, the Chinese people, and the Chinese nation. It is the leadership core for the cause of socialism with Chinese characteristics and represents the developmental demands of China's advanced productive forces, the orientation for

China's advanced culture, and the fundamental interests of the greatest possible majority of the Chinese people. The Party's highest ideal and ultimate goal is the realization of communism."[1]

Political civilization with the people as masters of their own country. This is the essence of socialist political civilization with Chinese characteristics. The supremacy of the people is the fundamental direction of political development and the fundamental trend of political modernization. The cardinal principles of the Constitution of the People's Republic of China (2018) make clear that the people are masters of their own country, that "All power in the People's Republic of China belongs to the people" (Article 2), and that all public affairs and activities must have affinity to the people. These are the essential requirements for all political affairs and activities in contemporary China, and the only basis for the legitimacy of all state systems and public governance.

Political civilization with the unity of the people's state system and system of government. China's political system features the unity of the people's state system and system of government, i.e., the people's democratic dictatorship led by the working class and based on the alliance of workers and peasants; and the system of people's congresses, the system of CPC-led multiparty cooperation and political consultation, the system of regional ethnic autonomy, and the system of community-level self-governance. The people's democratic dictatorship is China's state system; the system of people's congresses is China's system of government. The relationship between the state system and the system of government is that between content and form. The state system determines the system of government while the latter reflects the former, with relative independence. As Article 1 of the Constitution of the People's Republic of China (2018) stipulates, "The People's Republic of China is

---

[1] "Constitution of the Communist Party of China", accessed December 26, 2019, http://book.theorychina.org/upload/2017-19D-EN-2/

a socialist state governed by a people's democratic dictatorship that is led by the working class and based on an alliance of workers and peasants," which is the state system; as Article 2 of the Constitution of the People's Republic of China (2018) stipulates, "All power in the People's Republic of China belongs to the people. The National People's Congress and the local people's congresses at all levels are the agencies through which the people exercise state power," which is the political system.

The CPC leads the people in developing socialist democracy. According to the Constitution of the Communist Party of China (2017), "It shall preserve the organic unity of Party leadership, the running of the country by the people, and law-based governance, follow the Chinese socialist path of political development, expand socialist democracy, develop a socialist rule of law system with Chinese characteristics, and build a socialist rule of law country, thereby consolidating the people's democratic dictatorship and developing a socialist political civilization. It shall uphold and improve the people's congress system, the Communist Party-led system of multiparty cooperation and political consultation, the system of regional ethnic autonomy, and the system of public self-governance at the primary level. The Party shall develop a broader, fuller, and more robust people's democracy, advance extensive, multilevel, and institutionalized development of consultative democracy, and act in earnest to protect the people's right to manage state and social affairs and to manage economic and cultural matters. It shall respect and safeguard human rights. The Party shall encourage the free expression of views and work to establish sound systems and procedures for democratic elections, decision-making, administration, and oversight. It shall improve the socialist system of laws with Chinese characteristics and strengthen the implementation of law, to bring all the work of the state under the rule of law."[1]

Political civilization under democratic centralism. Democratic centralism is the fundamental organizational system and principle of China's politics and exercise of power. The Constitution of the People's Republic of China (2018) and the Constitution of the Communist Party of China (2017) both stipulate that democratic centralism is the Party's and the country's fundamental organizational principle and system. Central organs of public power and local organs at all levels, including Party and government bodies, state-owned enterprises (SOEs), and public institutions, are all strictly required to exercise power in a standard manner under the principle of democratic centralism, thus ensuring that the people's general will can be realized to the greatest extent in a democratic and centralized way. The political basis for unity of democracy and centralism is power's affinity to the people and serving the people.

Under the fundamental political system of the CPC's leadership and the people's supremacy, China's power structure consists of division of work, cooperation, and checks & balances of public power, led by the CPC, and with the people's primacy as the fundamental political purpose. In the power structure at the national level, the National People's Congress (NPC) is the highest organ of state power. Under it, there are legislative, judicial and administrative bodies to exercise state power. In the exercise of power within each organ, checks & balances are carried out between decision-making, executive and supervisory powers.

To advance political modernization, it is essential to uphold the unity of the CPC's leadership, the people's role as masters of their own country, and law-based governance; to strengthen institutional guarantees to ensure that the people have the controlling voice; to give play to the important role of socialist consultative democracy; to advance law-based

---

[1] "Constitution of the Communist Party of China", accessed December 26, 2019, http://book.theorychina.org/upload/2017-19D-EN-2/

governance; to further reform of Party and government institutions and the system of government administration; and to consolidate and develop the patriotic united front.

Guiding Principles for Political Progress

In progressing towards national rejuvenation, China must focus on combining fundamental issues of the CPC's leadership and the running of the country by the people, and promote the coordinated development of the people's democracy, rule of law, government and power. Emphasis should be laid on the following four issues:

—How to better advance the participation of the people as masters of their own country. Through the people's democracy, i.e. democracy of the majority, rather than concentration of power of the minority, China will do its best to ensure that the people are masters of their own country as they contribute to and gain from development in the people's republic, and promote national democracy, democracy at the primary level, and democracy in units and of citizens.

—How to better advance the rule of law. Through the people's rule of law, i.e. law-based governance by the majority, rather than autocracy of the minority, China will do its best to ensure that the people have the controlling voice, make further headway in the people's rule of law in the people's republic as they gain from development, and develop the rule of law at national and grassroots levels, in units, and by citizens.

—How to better advance public oversight over government. Through public oversight over government, i.e. majority oversight, rather than minority oversight, China will do its best to ensure that the people's governments at all levels fulfill the fundamental purpose of wholeheartedly serving the people, and constantly improve public services and administration.

—How to better advance power sharing by the people. Through the exercise of the people's power, which pursues majority rather than minority benefit, China will do its best to ensure that public power is exercised in public affairs and activities, and that power is conferred, exercised and governed by the people.

China will remain committed to the fundamental political direction, improve and develop the political system, and work to achieve a broader, fuller and more robust people's democracy. In doing so, the basic political tasks are to ensure that the people have the controlling voice, strengthen the vitality of the Party and the country, harness the people's enthusiasm, expand socialist democracy, and make China a growing socialist country under the people's democracy.

China will uphold the basic political principle, develop and improve the political system, and work to achieve a broader, fuller and more robust people's rule of law. In doing so, the basic political tasks are to build a country, government and society based on the rule of law, and improve the institutions, standards and procedures of socialist democracy.

China will maintain the political nature, develop and improve the political system of the people's government, and work to achieve a broader, fuller and more robust people's administration. In doing so, the basic political tasks are to constantly improve public services and administration of the people's governments at all levels, and move towards a stronger and more prosperous country, national rejuvenation, and people's happiness.

China will remain committed to the fundamental political purpose, develop and improve the political system, and work to achieve a broader, fuller and more robust people's power. In doing so, the basic political tasks are to put in place a mode for the exercise of public power which the people can benefit from and appraise through discussion, confine the exercise of power within an institutional cage – the key to which is in the people's hands – and ensure that all public power is exercised under the people's democracy and rule of law.

The action guide for political progress towards national rejuvenation is as follows:

First, China will develop and improve the CPC's role of leadership core in providing overall leadership and coordinating the efforts of all involved. Efforts will be made to improve the democratic, good, law-based, secured and institutionalized governance of the CPC, ensuring that the Party leads the people in effectively developing and governing the country. The Party provides overall leadership over public affairs and activities of all ethnic groups, sectors and regions; and coordinates the efforts of all involved in affairs and activities in economic, political, cultural, social and environmental fields, and in diplomacy and national defense.

Second, China will develop and improve the fundamental purpose of the Constitution that all power of the state belongs to the people. Efforts will be made to expand the people's orderly political participation at all levels and in all areas, to mobilize and organize the people to manage state, social, economic and cultural affairs in accordance with the law as extensively as possible, to extend the forms and means of the people's democracy, and to support and safeguard the people's supremacy in a larger range, to a greater extent, and at a higher level.

Third, China will develop and improve the fundamental principle of the people's rule of law and law-based governance. Efforts will be made to increase public awareness of the rule of law, and realize law-based administration of state affairs and protection of civil rights. China must pursue coordinated progress in law-based governance, exercise of state power, and government administration, and promote integrated development of the rule of law for the country, the government and society, so as to improve the institutions and legalization of public affairs and activities of the state and all aspects of social life.

Fourth, China will develop and improve the organizational and institutional strengths of democratic centralism. Efforts will be made to modernize the leadership, organization and management systems of public affairs and activities. The CPC will work hard to create a lively political environment featuring both centralism and democracy, both discipline and freedom, and both unity of will and personal sense of ease. China will continue to strengthen its confidence in the path, theory, system, and culture of socialist political progress with Chinese characteristics.

Fair Government & Higher Efficiency

China's government at all levels is a people's government, consisting of administrative organs under people's congresses. Serving the people is the fundamental political mission, duty and purpose of government administration. The core of government construction and development includes: continuing commitment to the people-centered philosophy of development; upholding the administrative idea of unification of administrative justice and administrative efficiency; focusing on the administrative performance goals of fairness & justice, integration of power & responsibility, and quality & efficiency; fully advancing progress in government functions, law-based government, and administrative divisions; and striving to build a service-oriented and law-based modern government that is clean, efficient and able to satisfy the needs of the people with improved structure and sound functions.

1. Modernizing Government Administration

The government is the executive organ of state power, the administrative organ of the state. The government's basic functions are to provide needed public services to the public and to conduct necessary public administration. As prescribed by the political civilization of modern government and its administration, power is conferred, exercised and governed by the people.

To modernize government administration and meet the requirement of building a service-oriented and law-based government, in accordance with the performance standards of administrative fairness, efficiency and sustainability, China must properly handle the important relationships between government and Party committee, between government and people's congress, between government and market, between government and society, between the government's own service and administration, between different departments of government agencies, and between superior and subordinate levels of government.

Making all-round efforts to reform government agencies. China will adopt a comprehensive approach to the setup of Party and government institutions, and ensure that powers are designated properly and that functions and duties are defined clearly both for the institutions themselves and their internal bodies. China will use various types of staffing resources in a coordinated way, develop a sound system of government administration, and improve the organic law for state institutions. The government needs to transform its functions, further streamline administration and delegate powers, develop new ways of regulation and supervision, and strengthen its credibility and performance, building itself into a service-oriented government able to satisfy the needs of the people. More decision-making power should be given to governments at and below the provincial level, and ways should be explored to merge Party and government bodies with similar functions at the provincial, prefectural and county levels, or for them to work together as one office while keeping separate identities. China will deepen the reform of public institutions to see that they focus on serving public interests, relieve them of government functions, keep them away from business activities, and let them run their own day-to-day operations while maintaining supervision over them.

Upholding the principle of administrative competition. China will improve the functions of modern government, by further streamlining administration and delegating power, improving regulation, upgrading services, and enhancing administrative efficiency, so as to inspire creativity and vitality throughout market and society. China will further reform to see that the government recruits competent employees and dismisses those who are incompetent, and that government officials are prepared for both promotion and demotion, thus enhancing the vitality and competitiveness of civil servants. Efforts will be made to strengthen the rule of law in government procurement, make it more transparent and market-based, and reduce the cost and improve the efficiency of government administration.

Upholding the rule of law in government administration. Efforts will be made to promote law-based administration and development of the rule of law for the government. China will improve the lists of powers and responsibilities and the management of the negative list, and clearly define powers and responsibilities between government and market and between government and society. Steps will be taken to deepen reform of the administrative approval system, minimize government involvement in operational matters relating to business, and reduce to a minimum the scope of government approval. China will streamline administration and delegate power in a more targeted and coordinated way, and deepen reform in the business sector, providing convenient services.

Work will be done to deepen reform of public institutions that undertake administrative functions, and relieve them of government functions.

Upholding the principle of administrative innovation. China will develop new forms of government services, and provide open, transparent, efficient, convenient, fair and accessible administrative and public services. Steps will be taken to promote the standardization of administrative approval, improve the processes and service standards of work that directly affects enterprises and the public, and optimize and integrate horizontal and vertical relations between different administrative departments. China will modernize and advance IT application in government administration, promote the initiative of Internet Plus Government Services, and make every effort to make government affairs public.

2. Modernizing Government Functions

The setup of government's functions depends on the balance of rights and obligations in the relationship between country, individual, and society. The existence of a state and the establishment of the government aim to protect individual rights and interests and maintain social stability. In reality, however, fulfillment of duties and national and social situations are subject to historical, economic, cultural and institutional constraints.

The functions of modern government mainly include providing public services and conducting public administration. Good government performance is reflected in two ways: first, the capacity to provide quality and affordable public services; second, the ability to conduct fair and righteous public administration. Government public services cover public welfare undertakings in education, healthcare, housing, infrastructure, culture, employment, elderly care, subsistence allowances, moral norms, legal aid, and humanistic care. Government public administration includes public administration of the economy, politics, culture, society, the environment, international affairs, and national defense.

Building a service-oriented government. The fundamental purpose of government is to serve the people, which is measured by the people's sense of fulfillment. To build a service-oriented government, it is essential to put people first and conduct government administration for the people, to improve the setup of functions to ensure that the people's government serves the people, and to serve the people in the practice of administration. The government should work to make itself clean and efficient with sound functions and improved structure, which is service-oriented and able to satisfy the needs of the people.

Promoting administration-oriented government. Modern government has important roles in both service and administration. Government administration includes both social and economic governance at the micro level, and regulation of aggregate and structure on a macro basis. Major tasks of macro-regulation are to keep the overall balance of the economy, coordinate major economic structure, optimize the distribution of productive forces, prevent or resolve the swings of the economic cycle, and prevent or resolve regional and systemic risks, thus achieving sound and sustained social and economic development.

3. Modernizing the Rule of Law for the Government

Building a law-based government is the key to building a country and society ruled by law. In building effective government towards national rejuvenation, China should focus on developing the rule of law for the government and promoting law-based government administration. The building of a rule of law government aims to develop new law enforcement mechanisms, improve the procedures of law enforcement, advance comprehensive law enforcement, and ensure strict law enforcement; to establish an authoritative and efficient system for law-based government administration that integrates power and responsibility; and to accelerate the building of a clean, efficient, open, impartial, honest and law-abiding government, with sound functions, statutory powers and responsibilities, and strict law enforcement.

Advancing law-based government administration. The rule of law is the life of government. In building a rule of law government towards national rejuvenation, the overarching objectives are to realize the rule of law in all elements and the entire process of government administration, seeing that the setting of power, the exercise of power, and checks on and oversight over the exercise of power are all law-based. China must perform the government's functions in all respects in accordance with the law, improve the legal system for administrative organizations and procedures, and legitimize administrative institutions, functions, power, procedures and responsibility. Steps should be taken to improve the procedures for major administrative decision-making, and improve mechanisms for law-based decision-making. China will advance reform of the system of administrative law enforcement, conduct comprehensive law enforcement of government administration, and improve the cohesive mechanisms of administrative law enforcement and criminal justice. Efforts will be made to see that law is enforced in a strict, procedure-based, impartial and non-abusive way, and to minimize discretionary power. China will put in place an evaluation system for all participants and the entire process of law enforcement, and improve the auditing system of government administration to safeguard the independent exercise of the power of supervision through auditing in accordance with the law.

Pursuing statutory administrative responsibility. In government administration, China must uphold the principles that all statutory duties must be performed, and that nothing should be done without legal authorization; China must have the courage to shoulder responsibility, and have the resolve to correct nonfeasance and malfeasance, overcome sloth in governance, and punish dereliction of duty. Government administrative organs must not designate power outside the law, or make any decisions outwith the basis of laws and regulations that might damage the legitimate rights and interests of citizens, legal persons and other organizations, or increase their obligations. China should establish the list of government power and eliminate the space for rent-setting and rent-seeking. Steps will be taken to ensure law-based and procedure-based exercise of powers by the government; improve the legal framework for powers of government at all levels, especially the central government and local governments; strengthen macro-administration, institutional functions and necessary law enforcement power of the central government; and adopt a holistic approach to ensuring equitable access to basic public services by provincial governments, and to the functions performed by governments at municipal and county levels.

Improving mechanisms for law-based decision-making. China will improve the government's administrative decision-making process, including public involvement, expert argumentation, risk assessment, review of legality, and collective discussion and decision, so as to ensure sound institutions, due process, transparent procedures, and clearly defined duties in administrative decision-making. Efforts should be made to establish and improve the mechanisms within government's administrative organs to review the legality of major decisions, as well as the system of government legal advisors. China needs to put in place sound mechanisms for lifelong accountability and investigation from the lowest to the highest level for major decisions, so that the chief executive and other leaders responsible for persons who made serious mistakes in decision-making, or made decisions not in a timely manner in accordance with the law, will be held accountable by law for causing significant losses and negative influence.

Creating a sound system for administrative law enforcement. China must promote rational allocation of the government's administrative law enforcement forces while upholding the principle of simplifying the administrative structure, integrating forces, and improving efficiency, in accordance with the responsibilities and functions of governments at different levels. Great energy should be devoted to comprehensively advancing the government's administrative law enforcement and reducing types of government's law enforcement teams. China will put in place a sound governance system for administrative law enforcement of local governments, rationalize the system of administrative enforcement, and move faster to build comprehensive law enforcement agencies for urban governance. China must strictly implement the system of employment with certificates and qualification management for administrative law enforcement personnel, and the system in which the administrative organ that makes the decision on a fine shall be separated from the organ that collects the fine. Efforts will be made to improve the connection between administrative law enforcement and criminal justice, as well as standards and procedures for case transfer, and develop the system to ensure information-sharing, case notification, and case transfer between administrative law enforcement, public security, procuratorial and judicial organs, thus realizing seamless connections between administrative and criminal penalties.

Checks and Oversight over the Exercise of Power

Power refers to a dominant force within the range of responsibility; state power is coercive force that dominates state affairs and activities in accordance with state law. To achieve national rejuvenation, questions such as the following are of fundamental importance: how to ensure all power in the PRC belongs to the people, how to put the exercise of power under the supervision of the people, and how to enable the people to benefit as much as possible from public power.

1. Upholding the View of Power on the Principal Status of the People: Improving the Principal-Agent Relationship of Public Power

People's view of power includes their general understanding of and attitude towards the source, the purpose, the exercise and the benefits of power, and scrutiny of the exercise of power. Of these, the questions of who is in power, who exercises power, who supervise the exercise of power, and who benefits from power are the most basic issues. At different stages of human society, in different social and political systems, and governed by different political parties, people have different or even opposite understandings in their view of state power.

Observing the purpose of the people's power. The view of power to which the CPC remains committed is a Marxist view of people's power, upholding that all power of the state belongs to the people and that the people are masters of state power. Any state power is the power of the people, which is entrusted, supervised and shared by the people without exception; any state power must give full expression to the will of the people, and the people's sense of fulfillment from the people's power must be maximized. Xi Jinping points out that in advancing the law-based governance of the country, China must focus on safeguarding and promoting social fairness and justice. Social fairness and justice is a lofty goal of the CPC. In order to serve the people wholeheartedly, the Party must pursue fairness, uphold justice, and protect the people's rights and interests.

Improving the principal-agent relationship of power. State power, deriving from the people, is however exercised by individuals. From the people to individuals, the problem of the principal-agent relationship of public power is of vital importance. It is crucial to ensure that the exercise of state power is for the people. This significant and practical issue is the most difficult to tackle in modern governance of public power.

To improve the principal-agent relationship of power, it is essential to ensure that there is nothing going wrong in the performance assessment, selection, management and dismissal of officials who hold power. China must resolve the question on how to advance intra-Party democracy and enable those who exercise power to represent the people as much as possible; the question on how to safeguard national democracy, and ensure that government officials appointed by local people's congresses at various levels do their best to serve the people; the question on how to select and appoint leading officials in Party and government organs, SOEs and public institutions, and enable them to fully express the will of the people, with true integrity and ability. The people alone are the source of power and justice.

Promoting fair exercise of power. First, China should enhance coordination and checks between intra-Party power and state power, and between legislation, judicature and administration at the national level. Second, China should enhance coordination and checks between decision-making power, enforcement power, and supervisory power. Only with coordination of and checks on the exercise of power can China ensure fairness in power and efficiency in administration. Third, China should skillfully balance the exercise of power and the fulfillment of responsibility, and handle the benefits and risks of power. China will put in place effective mechanisms for power allocation and the exercise of power to ensure that officials are prepared for both selection and dismissal, and both promotion and demotion, and that competition is fair and officials are honest, moving faster to modernize the allocation and exercise of power.

2. Upholding the View of Power on the People's Rule of Law: Modernizing the Rule of Law in Public Power

The view of power on the rule of law refers to thinking and ideas that define the boundaries, exercise and performance of power through well-conceived legal system, including the concept of statutory power, responsibility and assessment and of other legal rights. Statutory power means that government departments must not do anything unless it is mandated by the law. Statutory responsibility implies the symmetry between power and responsibility – Where there is power, there is an equivalent weight of responsibility, which must be shouldered. Statutory assessment refers to law-based performance assessment, rewards, and penalties.

At all times and in all countries, power without boundaries, responsibility or performance assessment, inevitably leads to abuse, lack of control, alienation and corruption, as well as bureaucracy and formalism. The root cause of bureaucracy is the imbalance of power and responsibility – power without responsibility and power without restraint. The root cause of corruption in power is the imbalance between benefits and risks – Power brings benefits, which are risk-free.

Ensuring the rule of law in the exercise of power. State power is a country's coercive power, having a dual nature, which is both positive and negative. Xi Jinping points out that power is a double-edged sword. It benefits the people when exercised in accordance with the law, but endangers the country and the people when exercised outside the law. To confine the exercise of power to an institutional cage, China must designate, discipline, restrict and supervise power in accordance with the law.

Every Party and government organization and every official must obey and abide by the Constitution and other laws. No one may use the Party's leadership as a pretext to override the law with their own arbitrary fiats, place their own power above the law, or bend the law for personal gain.

In order to ensure the rule of law in the exercise of power, China must ensure that power is exercised under public oversight and in broad daylight, and eliminate hotbeds of corruption in power. China should concentrate on standardizing leading officials' powers and responsibilities, putting in place sound accountability procedures and systems, strengthening economic responsibility audit of leading officials, improving the mechanisms to apply checks on the exercise of power inside government, and enhancing monitoring, auditing and supervision of the exercise of power.

Upholding the principle of power checks and balances. Power checks and balances is the most important philosophy in modern politics. Power imbalances are the root cause of all power corruption. Power checks and balances include checks and balances between legislation, judicature and administration, and between decision-making, enforcement and oversight, as well as top-down oversight in the power system, and horizontal restraint between deferent power sectors.

First, China should remain committed to "power constraining power". Any power has coercive effect. So does state power. The coercive effect of power must be constrained by an equivalent coercive effect, i.e., applying oversight and checks to the exercise of power by corresponding or even bigger power. Second, China should stay committed to "benefits regulating benefits". Power can bring benefits while great power can bring great benefits. Benefits brought by power must be regulated by corresponding benefits, especially material benefits in full, to inspire oversight over and management of the exercise of power.

To uphold the principle of power checks and balances, it is important to properly handle the relationship of checks and coordination of power. Power checks aim to avoid monopolist or uncontrolled power and prevent corruption and alienation of power; power coordination aims to avoid decentralization and confrontation of power, and prevent power inefficiency and incompetence. Taking decision-making power, enforcement power and supervisory power for example, the lack of distinction and checks & balances will inevitably lead to monopoly, corruption and alienation of power; domination without coordination will cause decentralization, inefficiency and incompetence of power.

To uphold the principle of power checks and balances, it is imperative to increase transparency in the exercise of power. Transparency is the key to just power while sunlight is the preservative of power. Only by continued efforts to increase transparency in the exercise of power can China ensure that state power is exercised within statutory authority and in accordance with statutory procedures; can China ensure that decision-making is sound, democratic and law-based, and improve mechanisms and procedures for decision-making; can China put in place sound systems for making Party affairs, government affairs and judicature more transparent; and can China strengthen intra-Party oversight, democratic oversight, legal oversight, and oversight through public opinion.

3. Pursuing the Exercise of Power under Public Oversight: Strengthening Oversight over the Exercise of Public Power

Power is the basis of politics while just power is the foundation of civilized politics. The farther power is removed from the public, the closer corruption is to the public; when power is exercised under public oversight, corruption is rare. China should pursue a holistic approach to oversight over the exercise of public power, by enhancing intra-Party oversight, oversight by people's congresses, democratic oversight, administrative oversight, judicial oversight, and oversight through auditing and public opinion. China should put in place sound and effective systems to check and supervise the exercise of power, increase synergy, and deliver outcomes.

To enhance oversight over the exercise of public power, it is crucial to ensure that the people wield power, that power is delegated by the people and exercised under public oversight, and that power benefits the people. Modern politics, power and civilization require that the people hold the key to power. In the PRC, the people are true masters of the country – All power of the state belongs to the people and is shared by the people.

First, China has put in place sound institutional organizations to ensure that the people wield and exercise power, including the system of people's congresses, the system of CPC-led multiparty cooperation and political consultation, the system of regional ethnic autonomy, and the system of community-level self-governance – All are fundamental, and all must be efficient. Second, China needs to establish and improve social systems to ensure that the exercise of power is governed by the people, is under public oversight and benefits the people, and needs to improve oversight by citizens, market organizations and news media.

To enhance oversight over the exercise of public power, it is crucial to provide incentives of interests. Incentive mechanisms are the fundamental driving force for all human activities. By developing various incentive mechanisms, China can coordinate interests and design public power to ensure that interests are shared by the majority of the people, which is the basic principle of social dynamics.

To coordinate interests through incentive mechanisms is to drive behavior by means of definite, adequate and practical benefits. Promoting social fairness and justice includes the anti-corruption campaign. In order to get bigger and more lasting results, China needs to carry out institutional reform and develop mechanisms to provide guarantees, i.e., giving fighters against corruption sufficient benefits and expectations, and offering the cause of justice rewards for ensuring justice. This is because any action against evildoers and evil deeds, especially serious corruption and criminal offences, is scarce social behavior with high risk. Fighters against corruption are faced with direct and indirect risks and pressures on their bodies and minds, families and careers, living in an unjust social environment and suffering pressure of public opinion, which as a general principle far exceed positive incentives. In these circumstances, without adequate and positive interests, for example, huge reward and commissions, it is impossible for a better social environment that upholds justice to take shape.

Putting in place a sound system to reward offence reporting. To encourage full participation in conducting oversight over the exercise of power, it is necessary to develop mechanisms with a long-term impact in which good is rewarded with good and evil is rewarded with evil. Only by doing so can good people and good deeds become the norm and evil persons and evil things be isolated. At all times in countries with a low incidence of corruption, good is rewarded with good, evil is rewarded with evil, and people have a high degree of participation in anti-corruption campaigns. In countries with a high incidence of corruption, the opposite is the case. Without mechanisms with a long-term impact, there will be no broad participation of the people, and no country will be able to curb power corruption.

Increasing transparency in the exercise of power. Sunlight is the best preservative. Making the exercise of power more open and transparent is essential to advancing the rule of law for the government, the country, and society. Xi Jinping stresses that opening government affairs is an important mechanism in China's efforts to build a rule of law government. Institutions should be developed to make public the whole process of government business, to ensure that where power is exercised there is transparency and oversight. China will fully advance transparency in government affairs, making decision-making, enforcement, administration, services and results more public.

Strengthening oversight over and checks on the exercise of administrative power by the government. China should focus on oversight over financial funds, state assets, public investment, government procurement, public resources, public projects, and other departments and positions with a concentration of power. Efforts should be made to exercise different power for different purposes, designate different power for different posts and at different levels, rotate posts regularly, and strengthen internal institutional supervision, so as to avoid abuse of power. China will improve hierarchical oversight and special oversight within the government, enhance oversight over lower bodies by higher ones, and put in place sound institutions to regularize oversight within the system. China will improve mechanisms for correction and accountability of public power, and improve accountability procedures. These include being ordered to make a public apology, being suspended from one's duties and receiving investigation, admitting mistake and resigning on one's own accord, being ordered to resign, and being dismissed. China will put in place a sound national auditing system, and ensure the independent exercise of power of oversight through auditing in accordance with the law. China will ensure full auditing coverage of public funds, state assets, state resources, and leading officials' fulfillment of economic responsibilities. China will strengthen the leadership of higher auditing bodies over lower ones, pursue unified management of personnel, funds and property of auditing bodies, and move faster to professionalize auditing processes.

Chapter 4

Cultural Modernization towards National Rejuvenation

Culture is a general term for activities involving the production of knowledge such as education, science and technology, and for mental activities and achievements, including ideology, morality and beliefs. Human civilization focuses on developing cultural programs and industries and creating a spiritual home. The level of cultural programs and industries, together with the capacity to build a spiritual home and moral beliefs, directly determines the level of a human society from the individual level through family, country, and nation. To realize national rejuvenation, China should give top priority to promoting cultural programs and cultural-ethical progress.

Cultural Modernization

Cultural confidence represents a fundamental and profound force that sustains a country and a nation. At present, there are 214 countries and regions in the world, inhabited by over 2,500 ethnic groups, who own more than 5,000 cultures and speak nearly 20,000 languages. With increasing globalization, marketization and IT application, global culture has entered an era of fusion and competition, witnessing integration and evolution, prosperity and decline, and emergence and extinction.

The Chinese nation, with a 5,000-year-long civilization, has created a splendid culture, not only nourishing its people, but also making an outstanding contribution to humanity. Faced with changing times, Chinese culture is experiencing the most drastic changes for thousands of years.

The Constitution of the Communist Party of China (2017) stipulates that "The Communist Party of China shall lead the people in developing advanced socialist culture. It shall promote socialist cultural-ethical progress, ensure the practice of the rule of law in combination with the rule of virtue, and work to strengthen the thinking and morality as well as the knowledge of science and culture of the whole nation, to provide powerful ideological guarantees, motivation and intellectual support for reform, opening up and socialist modernization, and develop a strong socialist culture in China."[1]

Modern developments in education, science & technology and culture are behind China's drive to achieve national rejuvenation. The central ideas of these developments are: making all-round progress in moderniz-

---

[1] "Constitution of the Communist Party of China", accessed January 2, 2020, http://book.theorychina.org/upload/2017-19D-EN-2/

ing education, fully implementing strategies to invigorate China through education and educational development, putting in place a modern educational system and a lifelong learning system, and building learning Party organizations, a learning society and a learning Party, so as to provide comprehensive and sustained intellectual impetus and resources for national rejuvenation.

The raising of intellectual, moral and cultural-ethical standards is the soul and the root of development for the Chinese nation. To realize national rejuvenation, priority should be given to fostering a Chinese spirit. China must promote humanistic care and cultural-ethical progress, and develop a system of institutions to raise intellectual, moral and cultural-ethical standards. Through comprehensive and sustainable institutional incentives and civilization, the Chinese people will achieve the goal of building a great modern socialist country with Chinese characteristics that has high intellectual, moral and cultural-ethical standards.

The core ideas of promoting cultural programs are: helping socialist cultural programs with Chinese characteristics to thrive, developing a public cultural service system that covers the whole society, and ensuring equitable access to public cultural services. China should develop cultural programs that serve the public interest, and guarantee the people's basic cultural rights. China will ensure government dominance in strengthening cultural infrastructure that serves the public interest and provides basic services with equitable and convenient access, in improving the network of public cultural services, and in increasing free cultural services. China should put in place a comprehensive public cultural service system, build a modern communication system, develop a system to carry forward the best of traditional Chinese culture, and coordinate cultural development in urban and rural areas.

The core ideas of developing cultural industries are: turning socialist cultural industries with Chinese characteristics into pillar industries of the economy, and enhancing the overall strength and international competitiveness of the national culture. China needs to put social benefits first while pursuing economic returns, and promote the leapfrog development of cultural industries. China needs to build a system for cultural industries, form a cultural industry development pattern in which public ownership plays a dominant role while entities under diverse forms of ownership develop side by side, promote cultural and technological innovation, and expand cultural consumption.

The core ideas of developing the cultural system are: creating a vigorous and efficient system of cultural management and mechanisms for production and operation of cultural products, and improving the cultural opening-up model to preserve Chinese culture, absorb foreign cultures, and help Chinese culture go global. China needs to develop a cultural management system that integrates government administration, industry self-discipline, public oversight, and law-based operation by enterprises and public institutions. China should pursue modern cultural enterprises and modern systems of cultural market & cultural management. The government needs to transform its functions, and give better play to its role of policy regulation, market oversight, social management, and public services. China will improve mechanisms to provide policy guarantees for cultural development, fully advance the globalization of Chinese culture, and carry out multilevel cultural exchanges with foreign countries through multiple channels and in various forms to draw on foreign cultural achievements.

The core ideas of developing cultural products are: meeting the people's needs for richer cultural products and more fine works. China should enable literature and art to serve the people and the building of socialism, encourage more lively exchanges of diverse cultures, and provide the people with richer intellectual nourishment. China will see that culture guides social ethos, educates the people, serves society, and promotes development. China will adhere to the right direction in literary and artistic creation, see philosophy and other social sciences thrive, enhance media work, develop a healthy Internet culture, and improve the evaluation system and incentive mechanisms for cultural products.

The core ideas of fostering cultural talent are: strengthening the competence of cultural talent, training professional personnel for socialist cultural programs, and turning China into a country strong in socialist talent. China needs to encourage high-performing cultural talent and high-level leading figures; improve the training of cultural talent that serve the grassroots, improve the work ethic and conduct of cultural practitioners, and implement the strategy on developing a quality cultural workforce nationwide.

To modernize cultural governance, China will ensure that culture serves the people and the building of socialism, encourage more lively exchanges of diverse cultures, and pursue innovative development. The priorities are summarized as follows:

- holding firmly the leading position in ideological work;
- cultivating and observing core socialist values;
- raising intellectual and moral standards;
- seeing socialist literature and art thrive; and
- developing cultural programs and industries.

Modernizing Education

The development of human society, including individuals, families, nations and countries, in the final analysis means the development of education. As long as education is developing, humanity has hope and a future. Modernizing China's education fundamentally determines national rejuvenation and the direction the civilization will take. China must show firm resolve in invigorating the country through education and in prioritizing educational development, improve the national educational and lifelong learning system, and enhance the quality of modern education, thus providing sustained motivation and intellectual support for national rejuvenation.

In 1949, the illiteracy rate of China's total population was more than 80%, with the figures for the rural population and the urban population being 95% and 70% respectively. The national enrollment rate for school-age children was less than 20%; only 13% of the population attended primary school; the educational poverty incidence reached 93% (the proportions of illiterate population and population at primary school level). In 2010, illiteracy had dropped to 4.08%; the proportion of population at primary school level was 26.78%; and the educational poverty incidence decreased to 30.86%. In 2010, in every 100,000 people, 8,930 had surpassed junior college degree, 14,032 were at the level of high school or technical secondary school, 38,788 at junior secondary education level, and 26,779 at primary school level.

Since reform and opening up in 1978, educational modernization has accelerated. In 1978, there were 598 institutions of higher education; in 2018, the figure reached 2,663, including 1,245 undergraduate institutions and 1,418 higher vocational (professional training) colleges. In 2018, there were 76,746 secondary schools, of which 24,320 were senior middle schools and 52,426 were junior middle schools; there were 170,209 primary education schools, of which 161,811 were regular primary schools and 8,398 were adult primary schools. China's gross enrollment ratio of higher education was 10 percentage points higher than the world average, although 30 percentage points lower than that of high-income countries.

China is currently transforming from a country of huge human resources to a country of quality human resources. In 1978, there were 856,000 college and university students; the figure increased to 5.561 million in 2000 and 28.31 million in 2018, growing at an average annual rate of 9.1% between 1979 and 2018. In 1978, there were 206,000 full-time teachers in institutions of higher learning; the figure jumped to 463,000 in 2000 and 1.673 million in 2018, growing at an average annual rate of 5.4% between 1979 and 2018. In 1978, there were 10,934 postgraduate students, with 10,708 new students and only 9 graduates; in 2000, there were 301,239 postgraduate students, with 128,484 new students and 58,767 graduates; in 2018, there were 2,731,257 postgraduate students, with 857,966 new students and 604,368 graduates.

Educational modernization has become the most important driving force for China's social and economic development. In 1992, expenditure on education was RMB86.7 billion, of which RMB72.87 billion came from the government. In 2018, expenditure on education was RMB4.3 trillion, including RMB3.4 trillion of funds allocated by the government, RMB22.5 billion spent on private education, RMB8.5 billion of social donations, RMB695.8 billion of undertaking revenue and RMB108.7 billion of other educational expenditure.

According to American scholar Robert W. Fogel, the No.1 driver of China's rapid economic growth is huge spending on education. He drew on US data to show that the productivity of graduate workers is three times that of those below junior middle school level and 1.8 times that of workers at senior middle school level.

In terms of workers' years of schooling, in 1950, the average years of schooling of China's population aged 15 years old and above was 1 year, 11.9% of the US figure; in 1980, the figure was 5.33 years, accounting for 44.3% of the US figure; in 2010, the figure was 9.9 years, accounting for 81.1% of the US figure.[1] In 2018, the average years of schooling of the working-age population in China was 10.5 years, and the average years of schooling of the new workforce was 13.4 years. At present, the educational level of workers in China still lags behind that of developed countries, especially in terms of the quality of education. The most prominent problem is that China's supply of technical and skilled personnel and craftsman is insufficient for a major country. According to statistics from the Ministry of Human Resources and Social Security, skilled workers account for one fifth of the national total of employees, and highly skilled personnel constitute less than 6% of the national total. Therefore, China faces a serious shortage of skilled talent in its modernization drive.

To achieve national rejuvenation, educational modernization includes the following missions: First, to meet the requirements of economic globalization, information socialization, and national modernization, China needs to fully reform educational modernization, improve the quality of education, and put in place a world-class modern educational system. Second, China needs to tackle the problems caused by unbalanced and inadequate development between urban and rural areas, between different regions, between schools and between families, and standardize education, ensuring equitable access and strengthening the rule of law. Third, to reform the quality of education and promote fairness in education, China needs to modernize the capacity-building of public school teachers and social educationalists, and concentrate the efforts of the country, enterprises, society and international forces on the development of modern education in China.

To realize national rejuvenation, educational modernization requires: First, increase the number of years of compulsory education and the

---

[1] Hu Angang & Yan Yilong: *China's National Conditions and Development*, Chin. ed., China Renmin University Press, Beijing, 2016, p. 214.

participation rate. China will integrate senior secondary education into compulsory education to bring the participation rate to world advanced level. Second, promote social education. China will step up efforts to build a learning society and learning organizations, and increase participation in social education to world advanced levels. Third, standardize the level of education, and train a large number of skilled and innovative people with strong personalities who pursue well-rounded development. Fourth, internationalize and globalize education and strengthen comprehensive exchanges with other countries, especially educationally developed countries. Fifth, increase IT application in education and build a great modern country with world-class online education.

Prioritizing the development of education. China needs to foster virtue through education, enhance well-rounded development of individuals, promote fairness in education, and nurture a new generation of capable young people who have a good and all-round moral, intellectual, physical and aesthetical grounding. China needs to put in place a modern comprehensive education system that provides multiple levels, types and forms of education, and further develop public education, social education and market-oriented education to meet the need for different levels of and different types of education.

Prioritizing the expenditure on and development of education. To encourage the allocation of more quality resources to the field of education, China must give priority to educational input and development, including government investment, preferential taxation, financial support, teachers' remuneration, and education security. Only by prioritizing education in the modernization drive can China provide inexhaustible intellectual support for the development of the country, society, and civilization. Priority should be given to educational development in the national social and economic development plan. China must ensure that government funds lay particular stress on education, and that public resources first meet the development needs of educational undertakings. Every effort will be made to improve the institutions, mechanisms and policies of revitalizing education, to encourage the development of private schools, and to keep expanding the involvement of social resources in various types of education.

Increasing the proportion of government spending on education. The international criterion for educational input is that government spending on education should account for 4% of GDP. At present, the world average is about 7%, with the figure in developed countries being 9%. In 2018, the figure on China's mainland was 3.58%. China will see that by 2049, the figure reaches the average level of developed countries. To achieve this, China needs to extend fiscal reform in all respects, and improve the structure of fiscal expenditure to ensure that government spending on education precedes all other expenditures.

Modernizing Science and Technology

Science and technology are the primary productive force, and the fundamental driving force for social and economic development. In China's endeavor to realize national rejuvenation, the scale, process, speed, quality and efficiency of technology modernization directly determine the stage, status, level and quality of national socio-economic development. Modernizing science and technology to build China's strength in science and technology is the No.1 strategic project of national rejuvenation.

1. Science and Technology as the Fundamental Force for Human Development

Science and technology are humanity's sharpest weapon in understanding and transforming the world. They manifest the different stages and levels of human civilization. The most fundamental differences between nomadic, agrarian, industrial and information civilizations, between developed and developing countries, and between advanced and backward countries are hierarchical differences in science and technology. The history of human society is first of all the history of technological progress.

In modern society, industrialization, driven by scientific revolution, has passed through the phases of steam technology, electric technology and information technology, and ushered in the era of the fourth scientific revolution which is represented by computer, Internet and information science, with artificial intelligence, clean energy, unmanned control, quantum information, virtual reality and biology engineering as the main constituents. In terms of modern production exchange and consumption, the fourth scientific revolution will guide humanity into a higher level of knowledge economy, network economy and information economy, with a trend towards smart manufacturing, smart products, smart services, smart management, the cloud factory, and web-based services.

In the future, world science will develop in depth at various scales, from the microscopic to the mesoscopic world, and from the macroscopic to the cosmological world. Massive technological innovation that is green, intelligent and ubiquitous is restructuring international industrial division. Some groundbreaking technological revolutions are brewing, which will reshape the global competitive landscape and change power structures among various countries. Technological innovation has become the core strategy of developed countries in seeking competitive strengths.

The future world trends of technological development are: First, digital science, network technology, and the Internet of Things will play a more and more important role in technological development. Second, biosciences and physical hardware technology will continue to enhance the functions of the human body. Third, innovative technology will provide new tools for adapting the physical environment, and strengthen the capacity of individuals and enterprises. Socio-technical innovations will better ensure citizens' rights and interests and improve public governance. Fourth, science and technology will provide more guarantees for health & safety in work and daily life.

2. Development Trends of China's Technological Modernization

As science and technology create productivity, the key to China's national modernization is technological modernization. In 1949, there were fewer than 50,000 scientific and technical personnel in China. By 1978, the figure had increased to 4.3 million, including 1.6 million engineers and technicians, 1.3 million health workers, 894,000 teachers, 294,000 agricultural technicians, and 320,000 scientific researchers.

Since 1979, China has accelerated its technological modernization. In 1980, China's technological strength accounted for 2.3% of the world total, while the US made up 24.6%; in 2010, China's technological strength accounted for 16.1% of the world total, and the US 22.7%. By 2010, China had become the No. 2 country worldwide in terms of technological strength. In 2019, China ranked 14th in the Global Innovation Index (GII), with its rankings improving in the indexes of system, human capital & research, infrastructure, knowledge & technology output, and creative output. According to the Analysis Report of National Technological Forecasting of Chinese and Foreign Competition, in China's current technological makeup, tracking technology accounts for 52%, parallel technology 31%, and leading technology 17%. The follow-up capacity of China's overall technological strength has improved significantly, with its overall level of technology accounting for 67% of that of the US.

Technological innovation has now been put in a core position in China's overall national development, playing an important and increasing supporting & leading role. In 2013, China's R&D investment accounted for more than 2% of GDP for the first time; in 2018, the figure increased to 2.18%, to which enterprises' contributed 70%, showing remarkably increasing innovation needs of enterprises. By the end of 2018, there were 181,000 high and new technology enterprises; the added value of high-tech products accounted for 16% of the total from industrial enterprises with an annual revenue of RMB20 million and above; the export of high-tech products reached US$743 billion. From 2013 to 2018, China's high-tech industries and strategic emerging industries, maintaining an average annual growth rate of over 10%, became new drivers of economic development. In 2018, advances in science and technology contributed 58.5% of national economic growth, giving a strong boost to industrial transformation and upgrading. Some industries, at the forefront of the world, have provided new space and blazed a new trail for China's high-quality development.

In terms of the number of internationally published scientific papers, in 1980, China accounted for 0.2% of the world total, and the US 39.7%; in 2000, China accounted for 3.7% of the world total, and the US 28.6%; in 2011, China accounted for 14.1% of the world total, and the US 30.1%. From 2006 to 2016, Chinese scientific and technical personnel published a total of 1.7 million contributions to international papers, ranking second in the world, with its most-cited papers (those in the top 1%) accounting for 12.8% of the world total and ranking third globally. There were more than 1,500 foreign research institutions, making China one of the major forces in attracting and gathering global innovation resources. In 2017, China became the largest source country of global patent applications, industrial product designs, and trade mark.

In terms of patent applications and authorized patents, China has transformed from a blank space into a net exporter. In 1985, the number of PCT (Patent Cooperation Treaty) patent applications from China accounted for 0.01% of the world total; the US accounted for 35.7%. In 2012, the State Intellectual Property Office accepted 653,000 patent applications from home and abroad, accounting for 27.8% of the world total and exceeding the figure of the US which was 23.1%. Of these, residents' patent applications totaled 561,000, surpassing Japan and the US and leading the world for the first time. In 2000, 13,000 invention patent applications were authorized; this figure jumped to 432,000 in 2018, representing an average annual growth rate of 21.7%.

In terms of R&D investment, China's expenditure has continued to increase since 2000, serving as a determining factor for advancing technological innovation and making China the fastest growing country in this field. From 2000 to 2018, R&D expenditure increased from RMB89.6 billion to RMB1.97 trillion, an average annual growth rate of 18.7%. Registering high resilient growth in investment on science and technology, China ranks second worldwide in R&D investment.

According to *China Statistical Yearbook 2019*, there were 4.4 million full-time equivalent (FTE) R&D personnel in 2018, of whom 305,000 were doing research in basic science, 539,000 studying applications, and some 3.5 million in experimental development. Of 780 million workers in China, intellectual and skilled talent exceeded 150 million. Expenditure on R&D was RMB1.6 trillion, accounting for 2.19% of GDP. With regard to technological output and achievements in 2018, 1.84 million scientific papers and 53,629 other scientific works were published; 65,720 scientific and technological achievements were registered; and 67 National Awards for Technological Invention and 173 National Awards for Science and Technology Progress were given. About 4.3 million patent applications were accepted, including over 1.5 million applications for invention patents; and some 2.4 million patents were authorized, of which over 0.4 million were invention patents.

With regard to the proportion of high-tech export products in the world total, in 1980, China's figure was 0.03% while that of the US was 870 times higher; in 2010, China's figure was 20.4% which surpassed the US figure by a factor of 1.42 and the corresponding figures for the EU and Japan by 1.3 and 3.4. In 2018, imports and exports of high-tech products totaled US$1.41 trillion, of which exports represented US$743 billion and imports US$665.5 billion; the technology transactions totaled RMB1.77 trillion.

China's major problems in technological innovation are: Scientific and technological foundations are still weak, and innovation capability, especially in original innovation, is not strong; China still has to depend on other countries for core technologies in key fields; many industries remain at the middle or low end of global value chains; innovation makes a relatively low contribution to economic growth. There are still ways of thinking, ideas, systems and mechanisms that hinder innovative development, and the overall efficiency of the innovation system is relatively low. High-caliber leadership talent and highly-skilled personnel are urgently needed, and the innovative entrepreneurial ranks must be expanded. Great energy must be devoted to improving the incentive environment for innovation, implementing suitable policies and measures, opening and sharing innovation resources among more people, and promoting the spirit of science and innovative culture.

To achieve national rejuvenation, China's strengths in promoting technological innovation are:

First, with strong leadership and governing capacity the CPC can provide overall leadership, coordinate the efforts of all involved, and continue to create new thinking and new strategies for innovation-driven development.

Second, coordinating the strengths of socialism with Chinese characteristics, China can mobilize and organize all social resources to the greatest extent to implement the innovation-driven development strategy.

Third, upholding national incentives which put people first and focus on innovative talent, China can stimulate innovative systems and mechanisms through continuous reform.

Fourth, by pursuing independent technological innovation based on national conditions, and following a path of innovation-driven development that actively absorbs the wisdom and resources of global innovation, China can make overall progress in innovation models at different levels and in different directions, including introduction, imitation, integration, creation, surpassing and leading.

3. Technological Innovation Strategies towards National Rejuvenation

In modernizing science and technology, China aims to become a country strong in technological innovation, an important global center of technological innovation, and a leader in innovation. To realize national rejuvenation, China must solve the following key problems in modernizing science and technology:

First, China needs to reform, improve and modernize systems, mechanisms, policies, laws and regulations, in accordance with the requirements of a world-class technological country, and create an incentive environment for high-quality and high-level scientific research and technological innovation, and a humanistic environment that respects knowledge, encourages innovation and rewards scientific research.

Second, China needs to reform, improve and modernize the management of science and technology. China will put in place efficient and effective management systems to serve modern scientific research and technological innovation.

Third, China needs to focus on training and using talent for technological innovation, develop a high-intensive and market-based talent competition mechanism, and create a social, political and cultural environment that values and encourages innovation. Steps will be taken to build an efficient system for competition and selection of talent, a high-quality and market-based income distribution system that gives priority to talented people, and a high-quality incentive system for scientific research personnel.

By 2035, China will become an important source of technological innovators and establish a basic national innovation system with Chinese characteristics. First, an innovative economic structure will take shape; innovative approaches will be adopted to development; and main industries will operate at the medium-high end of the global value chain. Second, the independent innovation ability will be enhanced, and technological innovation will no longer be dominated by tracking. Third, the innovation system will be more collaborative and efficient; the national innovation system will be more complete; and science and technology will be deeply integrated with the economy and mutually reinforcing. Fourth, the innovative environment will be improved; a strong cultural atmosphere of innovation will take shape; rule of law will be strengthened to protect innovation; a dynamic situation highlighting creativity will be created; and socio-economic development and international competitiveness will be significantly improved.

By the 2050s, China will become a strong country in technological innovation and an important center of science & technology, with a number of first-class research institutes, research universities and innovative enterprises, and will gather high-caliber global personnel to create innovations and start businesses; technology and talent will become the most important strategic resources for national prosperity, and innovation will become the core factor in policymaking and institutional structuring; increases in labor productivity and strengthening social productive forces will rely mainly on technological progress and innovation, and the contribution of science and technology to the quality of economic development, consumption of energy resources, and core competitiveness of industries will reach the level of leading world powers; the institutional, market and cultural environments will be improved to promote innovation, while respect for knowledge, advocacy of innovation, protection of property rights, and inclusiveness and diversity will become the common ideals and value orientation of the public, which will provide powerful technological support for building China into a great modern socialist country that is prosperous, strong, democratic, culturally advanced, harmonious and beautiful, and for realizing the Chinese Dream of national rejuvenation.

To achieve national rejuvenation, China will take the following strategic steps to promote innovative development and modernize science and technology:

First, China will remain committed to supporting major national needs as a strategic task. China will give full play to the important role of technological innovation in fostering and developing strategic emerging industries, in improving the quality and efficiency of growth and upgrading the economy, in shaping leading-edge development, and in safeguarding national security.

Second, China will intensify efforts to catch up and take a lead in technological development. China will work to keep up with frontier development trends in world science and technology, improve its capacity for independent innovation, and seize the strategic initiative in a new round of global technological competition.

Third, China will pursue technological development for the benefits of the people as a fundamental purpose. China will focus on the vital interests and urgent needs of the people, and see that technological innovation plays a key role in improving the people's lives, in raising their cultural and health levels, in increasing employment, in promoting entrepreneurship, in reducing and eradicating poverty, and in building a resource-conserving and environment-friendly society.

Fourth, China will further reform as a powerful driving force for development. China will reform the scientific and technological system while advancing social and economic reform, and see that the market plays the decisive role in allocating resources and the government plays its role more effectively, so that technology management and operation mechanisms will take shape and remain lively.

Fifth, China will adopt a talent-driven approach to development. China will make human resource development a top priority for technological innovation, and train a large number of high-caliber, creative scientists and technicians.

Sixth, China will build a global vision on innovation. China will improve and allocate its innovative resources on a global scale, carry out cooperation on technological innovation at a higher level, endeavor to become a torchbearer in important fields and an important contributor to the international rules, and ensure that the country has its say in the global governance of innovation.

China should create a humanistic environment that inspires technological innovation. Karl Marx said, "There is no royal road to science, and only those who do not dread the fatiguing climb of the steep paths have a chance of gaining its luminous summits."[1] Greater innovation de-

---

[1] Karl Marx: "Preface to the French Edition", accessed January 8, 2020, https://www.marxists.org/archive/marx/works/1867-c1/p2.htm

mands a scientific, humanistic and social environment that is more modern and more universal. China must cultivate a comprehensive spirit of science and humanistic feelings. The spirit of science means pursuing science and truth, seeking truth from facts and the philosophy of science, and being pragmatic, scrupulous and down-to-earth. To have humanistic feelings is to put people first, be kind to others, and uphold humanity.

Building a Spiritual Home

As society and the economy develop and people's lives improve, their intellectual needs are becoming more and more important, as are those of wider society and the country. To realize socialist modernization and revive the Chinese civilization, it is essential to build a modern humanistic environment, which is vital for national rejuvenation and the people's happiness.

1. Modernizing Cultural and Ethical Progress

The Chinese people have fostered cultural traditions and moral values through thousands of years of historical development, forming the distinctive characteristics of a spiritual home for the nation. In building this spiritual home, the Chinese people pursue filial piety and personal integrity, show sincere feelings for each other and the motherland, foster a vision of inclusiveness, and aim to make a contribution to humanity. The Chinese civilization puts people first and promotes harmony.

To achieve national rejuvenation, a number of critical questions must be answered:

- how to adapt to opportunities and challenges brought by industrialization, urbanization, marketization, socialization, IT application, and globalization;

- how to respond to risks and challenges posed by competition, contest, disintegration, and conflict;
- how to achieve higher quality and higher level of cultural and ethical progress; and
- how to build a common spiritual home for the nation.

Promoting core socialist values. No individual can prosper without virtues, nor can any country. Core values, a fundamental driver of the texture and orientation of a culture, carry the spiritual aspirations of a nation or country, and represent the standard for judging right and wrong. As Xi Jinping pointed out, without shared core values, a nation or country will have no fixed abode for its soul, and its people will have no code of conduct to follow. Core socialist values represent the contemporary Chinese spirit and crystalize the values shared by all Chinese people. They determine the future of China, Chinese society, and Chinese citizens – a modern country that is prosperous, strong, democratic, culturally advanced and harmonious, a modern society that is free, equal, fair and law-based, and modern citizens that are patriotic, dedicated, honest and friendly.

Raising the intellectual and moral standards of the people. China will help its people raise their political awareness and moral standards, foster appreciation of fine culture, and enhance social etiquette and civility. China will undertake extensive activities to help the people develop firm ideals and convictions, build their awareness of socialism with Chinese characteristics and the Chinese Dream, foster a Chinese ethos and a readiness to respond to the call of the times, strengthen the guiding role of patriotism, collectivism and socialism, and see that the people develop an accurate understanding of history, ethnicity, country and culture. China will launch a civic morality campaign to raise public ethical standards, and enhance work ethics, family virtues and personal integrity. China will encourage individuals to strive for excellence and to develop stronger virtues, respect the elderly, love their families, and be loyal to the country and the people. China will improve and strengthen the ideological and political work, and launch initiatives to raise the public's cultural-ethical standards. The country will promote the spirit of science and make scientific knowledge widely accessible; the country will work to see the back of outdated social mores and to promote good and up-to-date practices and trends; the country will resist the corrosive influence of backward and decadent culture. China will institutionalize volunteer services, and heighten people's sense of social responsibility, awareness of rules and sense of dedication.

Building a shared ideal of socialism. This is the principal topic in promoting core socialist values and the spiritual impetus for China's rejuvenation. It is essential to uphold the national spirit advocating love of the country and follow the call of the times for reform and innovation. The shared ideal of socialism with Chinese characteristics helps strengthen national dignity, confidence, and pride; the socialist maxims of honor and disgrace helps promote public morality, work ethics, family virtues, and personal integrity; and the best of traditional Chinese culture helps foster a growing sense of cultural identity among the Chinese people.

Keeping fine traditional Chinese culture alive. The best of traditional Chinese culture features benevolence, people-centered philosophy, integrity, righteousness, concordance, and harmony. It showcases the Chinese nation's worldview, outlook on life, values, and aesthetic views formed in work and life and passed down through generations, the core of which has become the fundamental components of Chinese culture. These cultural features distinguish the Chinese nation from other nations, such as pursuing self-cultivation and working for the common good, making adaptations as times evolve and as circumstances change, and successfully handling affairs in accordance with the truth of all things on earth.

2. Building a Spiritual Home for the Chinese People

National rejuvenation is a process in which new heights are reached in every material, cultural, ethical and institutional dimension. It is also a process in which the people contribute to and gain from development, work for common prosperity, and create a better life. In building a spiritual home, China should adapt to the people's aspiration for a better life, and synchronize it with a drive to modernize the civilization that moves with the times – China needs to train well-educated citizens with high ethical standards, firm ideals and strong awareness of the rule of law, raise their intellectual and moral standards, and improve their cultural life.

The Chinese nation will promote the enterprising spirit, including thoughts, ideas and values such as "Constantly seek self-improvement" and "Reform and innovate".

The Chinese nation will foster intellectual nourishment for state governance, including the thoughts, ideas and concepts such as "Maintain unity of humanity and nature", "All under heaven belongs to the people", "The people are the foundation of the country", "The same water that keeps a ship afloat can also sink it", "Be on guard against adversity while cherishing peace", "Military forces are to be used only for the maintenance of peace and order", "Do things for the good of others", "Do not do to others what you do not want others to do to you", "Moral discipline and penalty are complementary measures to maintain social order", "Peace is of paramount importance", and "Seek harmony without uniformity".

The Chinese nation will improve its cultural and ethical values such as "The benevolent loves others", "Those who love and respect others will be loved and respected in return", "Do reverence to the elders in your own family and extend it to those in other families; show loving care to the young in your own family and extend it to those in other families", and "We appreciate our own culture along with other cultures so that all cultures flourish in harmony".

The Chinese nation will carry forward its traditional virtues, including social responsibilities of serving the country with selfless loyalty and "The country comes before the family, public interest comes before personal gain"; social norms of esteeming virtues, performing good deeds, and emulating virtuous people; and moral values of filial piety, fraternal duty, loyalty, honesty, courtesy, and righteousness. All these have a subconscious influence on the Chinese people's way of thinking and behavior. The Chinese people need to promote their traditional virtues such as working hard and enjoying company, helping others who are in poverty or difficulty, and acting bravely for a just cause.

The Chinese nation will uphold its humanistic spirit, reflected in the philosophies of seeking common ground while respecting differences, boosting culture to cultivate the people, and living a simple, disciplined and balanced life. China needs to advocate culture and thought that promote social harmony and encourage its people to strive for excellence.

The Chinese nation will build stronger cultural confidence. It has created a time-honored and brilliant culture during its 5,000-year history. No other country has suffered such oppression or disasters as China. Only by strengthening their cultural confidence can the Chinese people realize national rejuvenation.

The Chinese nation will develop a stronger sense of China as a major country. Since ancient times, China has been a populous country inhabited by a variety of ethnic groups. Its vast territory, long history, huge population and brilliant culture have created a sense of inclusiveness —

China takes the whole world as one community and pursues universal harmony. To make China one of the world's culturally developed countries, it is critical to modernize Chinese culture on a global basis, for the benefit of humanity, and towards a better future.

Chapter 5

Socialist Modernization towards National Rejuvenation

To build a more equitable, righteous, amiable and harmonious social civilization is a major component of the rejuvenation of the Chinese nation. In building such a social civilization, China will stay people-centered, uphold the concept of humanity, follow the principles of being equitable, righteous and amiable, and seek to protect livelihoods and social harmony. China will modernize its social structure, social security, social equity and social safety in all respects.

Social Civilization

Heading towards national rejuvenation, China is building a social civilization that parallels the rapid development of a new type of industrialization, urbanization, marketization, IT application, socialization, and internationalization. This is a period of diversified interests, multiple choices and ever-changing ideas, confronted with multi-tiered conflicts, social stresses and risks. Social modernization should particularly address pressing issues in social structure, social service, social security, and social safety.

1. Promoting Social Civilization on the Basis of Equity and Justice

Social civilization is the value compass of social development, the core of which is social equity and justice. The concept of social civilization, concerning a beautiful homeland, workspace, nation and world, is rooted in the equity and justice of social development, including equity in the system of rights and opportunities, equity in education, healthcare and housing, and equity in employment protection and development. Equity and justice are the core of a civilized society and the fundamental guides to the analysis and study of social issues.

Equity and justice are the core values of human civilization. In the long human history, every country, nation or society, regardless of its phase of development, path or social system, regarded equity and justice as a fundamental, systemic, basic and original issue. To purse equity and justice is the motivation for human civilization, progress, and harmony.

The government is thus required to continuously improve social equity and justice while developing public services and social security. Heading towards modernization in 2049, a new era when the Chinese people are working together for shared and common prosperity, China will enhance social equity and justice to better modernize social civilization, revitalize the nation, and create a better life for the people.

2. Creating Happiness by Improving Quality of Life

Quality of Life reflects the level of social civilization. To raise people's living standards and quality of life is the fundamental purpose of China's social development. To achieve national rejuvenation, China must bear this fundamental issue in mind.

Living standards, as one element of quality of life, involve the quantity and quality of the goods and services that the public have available to them. To a large extent, these fulfill the public's need for material goods, and living standards are mainly measured by per capita income or per capita consumption. Quality of life goes beyond per capita income and consumption and reflects the satisfaction of a wider group of needs, including material, cultural and social needs, the quality of living space, health services, education, the environment, social affairs, democracy, law-based governance, and human rights protection.

3. Promoting Social Development on the Basis of Life Satisfaction

"Life satisfaction" is a collective concept that refers to self-evaluation and personal feelings about life, experiences, physical and mental condition, work, and living and social environments. It is measured by three major indicators – satisfaction with material life, cultural life, and social life. Resolution 66/281, adopted by the 66th UN General Assembly on

June 28, 2012, proclaimed March 20th the International Day of Happiness, pointing out that "the pursuit of happiness is a fundamental human goal" and recognizing "the relevance of happiness and well-being as universal goals and aspirations in the lives of human beings around the world".[1] The World Happiness Report published by the UN measures a happiness index based on 33 items in 9 areas – education, health, environment, management, time, cultural diversity and inclusiveness, community vitality, inner happiness, and living standards. The report adjudges that proper public services, such as social environment, living and residential services, social trust, healthy lifestyles and growth quality, are crucial factors to drive up happiness indicators.

As China's economy and society progress, the Chinese people will have higher requirements for quality of life, such as health, food safety, clean water and air, satisfaction, and a sense of happiness. They will also have higher requirements for social civilization, such as social equity and justice, humanity, the rule of law, and security. A higher level of social speech, trust, support, participation and care has become an increasingly important element of their quality of life.

Developing China's life satisfaction index is critical to its social development. This index requires a comprehensive analysis through multiple dimensions, tiers and indicators, and effective exploratory research from diverse cognitive angles. From a personal perspective, the Human Development Index (HDI) can be generalized into three areas: the quality of people's material life and natural environment, the quality of people's spiritual and cultural life, and the quality of people's political and legal rights. From the nation's perspective, the HDI can be summarized into the following six areas: economic development and its equity, political

---

[1] "Resolution adopted by the General Assembly on 28 June 2012: 66/281. International Day of Happiness", accessed January 13, 2020, https://happinessday.org/wp-content/uploads/2015/11/UN66281.pdf

development and its equity, cultural development and its equity, social development and its equity, ecological development and its equity, and security development and its equity.

4. Building a Harmonious Society by Improving Living Standards

A harmonious society represents a set of favorable social conditions where all the members can display their abilities, find a suitable place, and live in harmony. China values the idea of harmonious society and proposes harmony between man and nature, man and society, and man and man. China also treasures other approaches to harmony, including filial piety, sincerity, kindness, morality, law, interest, righteousness, and impartiality. China advocates the harmonious thought of being dialectical which believes in harmony between heaven and earth and difference within harmony. Many great ancient Chinese thinkers expressed their thoughts on harmony. According to Lao Zi[1], man is an integral part of nature, and the Tao follows the law of nature. The *Book of Songs (Shi Jing)*[2] wrote that if one appreciated the virtues of a gentleman, all would be in harmony. Confucius[3] held the idea that harmony is precious and peace and accord breed harmony, while the decent man pursues harmony without uniformity. Mo Zi[4] pursued universal and undifferentiated love.

---

[1] Lao Zi (dates unknown), also known as Li Dan and Li Er, was a philosopher and the founder of philosophical Taoism in the Spring and Autumn Period (770-476 BC). – *Tr.*

[2] *The Book of Songs (Shi Jing)* was the earliest collection of poems in China. It contains 305 poems collected over some 500 years from the early Western Zhou Dynasty (c. 11th century-771 BC) to the middle of the Spring and Autumn Period (770-476 BC). – *Tr.*

[3] Confucius (551-479 BC), also known as Kong Qiu and Zhongni, was a philosopher, educator, statesman and the founder of Confucianism in late Spring and Autumn Period (770-476 BC). – *Tr.*

[4] Mo Zi (dates unknown) was the founder of Mohism in late Spring and Autumn Period (770-476 BC) and early Warring States Period (475-221 BC). – *Tr.*

Mencius[1] advocated extending the respect of the elderly and the love of the young in one's family to others.

Amid the gigantic universe, people are the top priority. In a harmonious society, people's quality of life is the foundation. As China is heading towards 2049, building a harmonious society means promoting people-centered development. Development needs to remain centered on people and quality of life. To ensure social equity and justice, China will properly deal with complex social interest relations and social stresses. By enhancing social assistance, China will create a stronger sense of gain among the people and enable them to benefit more from social development. Practicing the rule of law and good governance, China will improve the institutions for social development, to ensure the people's access to education, employment, medical services, elderly care, housing, and social assistance. China will facilitate the all-round development of people.

In building a harmonious socialist society, China should follow the principle of democracy and the rule of law, equity and justice, honesty and amiability, vitality, stability and order, harmony between man and nature, joint contribution and shared benefits. China will focus on guaranteeing and improving people's wellbeing and address the most pressing, most immediate issues that concern the people the most, so that development can better benefit all the people in a more equitable way. It is essential to improve public security and punish crimes and criminals that harm national security, national interests, social stability, and economic development. China pursues a holistic approach to national security, and stands firm in safeguarding its sovereignty, security and development interests.

---

[1] Mencius (c. 372-289 BC), also known as Meng Ke and Ziyu, was a philosopher and educator in mid-Warring States Period (475-221 BC). – *Tr.*

Building a Balanced Social Structure

A balanced social structure is the foundation of social progress. To achieve national rejuvenation, China must first achieve a balanced social structure in its efforts to promote social progress and prevent and reduce structural stresses resulting from the vested interests of different members of society. China should prevent and resolve points of stress in the relationships between social groups. China must work hard to solve the structural problems relating to population, urban-rural and regional imbalances, and disparities in wealth. And China must lay the foundations to improve social etiquette and civility and achieve better quality and more efficient social progress.

1. Balancing the Population Structure

Population, and particularly demographic problems are basic issues in national development and key to social progress and governance. Driven by increasing industrialization, urbanization, socialization, IT application, marketization and internationalization, China's population will change in terms of birth rate, size, structure and attributes. This will profoundly influence China's future development, modernization, and governance.

Population is a basic issue of strategic importance to China's sustainable development. In around 2,000 BC, there were approximately 10 million people in China; in AD 1 during the Western Han Dynasty, China had a population of 59.6 million, accounting for 25.8% of the world total; in 1110 during the Northern Song Dynasty, Chinese population was 120.7 million; in 1566 during the Ming Dynasty, the figure rose to 166.3 million; and in 1820 during the Qing Dynasty, the figure reached 381 million, peaking at 36.6% in terms of the proportion in the world total.

A comparative analysis of the population trend in China: In 1949, the population on China's mainland was 542 million, accounting for 21.5% of the world total; in 1979, the figure was 975 million, accounting for 22.3% of the world total; in 2019, the figure reached 1.4 billion, accounting for 18.2% of the world total. The United Nations predicted in 2013 that the population on China's mainland would grow to 1.45 billion in 2030, accounting for 17.2% of the world total; the figure would subsequently reduce to 1.38 billion, accounting for 14.5% of the world total. According to the UN report, "World Population Prospects: The 2015 Revision", in 1950 the respective populations of China, India and the US were 540 million, 410 million and 170 million; China's population will peak at 1.42 billion between 2030 and 2040; India's population will peak at 1.7 billion between 2050 and 2060; the American population will grow slowly to 420 million in 2100.

To revitalize the Chinese nation, China should focus on the size, attributes and structure of its population, especially the aging population. A society is classified as "aging" when over 7% of its people are aged 65 and above. If this proportion exceeds 14%, the society is a serious aging one; if it is greater than 20%, the society is a super-aging one. In 1982, the proportion of the aging population in China was 4.9% and the old-age dependency ratio was 8%; in 2000, the proportion of the aging population was 7%, and the old-age dependency ratio was 9.9%; in 2018, the proportion of the aging population was 12.6%, and the old-age dependency ratio was 18.1%. Within this figure, the disabled and semi-disabled elderly exceeded 40 million. Since 2000, China has become an aging society which is getting old before achieving prosperity. The UN population database predicted in 2012 that China's aging population would reach 23.9% in 2050, of which those aged 80 and above would account for 6.5%.

To realize national rejuvenation and achieve a balanced population,

China should focus on attributes, age demographics and regional distribution. Steps should be taken to improve the size, structure, attributes and distribution of population, and coordinate the development of population, resources, environment, the economy and society. China's main strategies include: adopting the right approach to population development, improving population development policies, and balancing the population structure.

2. Balancing the Urban-Rural Structure

Modernization is the process of transformation from an agricultural to an industrial civilization, and from a rural to an urban society. It is also the process of transfer from an agricultural and rural population to an industrial and urban population. In the endeavors to revitalize the Chinese nation, the ultimate approach to more balanced urban and rural development is coordinated industrialization, urbanization, agricultural modernization and IT application. China should strike a balance between agricultural and industrial development, between rural and urban dwellers, and between rural and urban areas. China should work to bridge the urban-rural structural divide as a priority and ensure equal treatment between urban and rural residents.

China will ensure equitable access to public services in urban and rural areas. To promote this equality is a process of coordinating economic, political, cultural, social and environmental development in city and countryside. It calls for comprehensive overall studying and planning of industry and agriculture, city and countryside, and urban and rural residents. Through deeper structural reform and policy adjustment, China will strive to ensure more equitable, standardized and law-based access to economic growth, industrial development, social information, infrastructure, environmental protection and social undertakings in urban and rural areas, to promote policy equality, industrial complementarity and consistent welfare in urban and rural areas, and to advance integrated, balanced, coordinated and sustainable social and economic development in city and countryside.

China will speed up work on granting permanent urban residency to people who move from rural to urban areas. In 1949, the proportion of urban residents on China's mainland was 10.6%; in 1979, 18.9%; in 2009, 48.3%; and in 2019, 60.6%. According to relevant UN studies, the proportion of urban residents on China's mainland will hit 70% in 2035, 75% in 2050, 80% in 2060, and over 85% in 2090.

China will advance rural modernization. Rural (including agricultural) modernization is the foundation of overall modernization in China. In this drive, it is essential to develop modern agriculture and rural industries, and improve the quality of rural public services and facilities. The key is to balance public resource allocation in rural and urban areas, and coordinate urban and rural modernization as a priority. The priority is to ensure that industry helps agriculture and that cities support the countryside, and implement the policy of "giving more, taking less, and loosening control" to increase rural incomes. All-round efforts should be made to coordinate economic, social, cultural and political development in urban and rural areas, and build rural areas with thriving businesses, social etiquette and civility, pleasant living environments and effective governance and prosperity.

3. Balancing the Regional Structure

With a large population and a vast territory, China's regional development is unbalanced. It is characterized by significant gaps in geography, population, resources, and social and economic development. Especially with its rapid industrialization, urbanization, marketization and internationalization, the imbalance in development between regions and within regions is growing, a phenomenon that seriously affects and constrains the overall modernization of the country. In the endeavors to revitalize the Chinese nation, it is of vital importance to achieve rational distribution of economic, political, cultural and social resources, to make plans for growth engines, clusters and belts for regional economies, and to coordinate regional social and economic development.

At present, China can be divided into four geographic and economic regions – the eastern, central, western and northeastern regions. In 2018, China's mainland population was spread as follows: eastern 38.5%; central 26.6%; western 27.2%; and northeastern 7.7%. The respective figures for GDP were 52.6%, 21.1%, 20.1%, and 6.2%.

In implementing the master strategy for regional development, guided by the Belt and Road Initiative, the coordinated development of the Beijing-Tianjin-Hebei region, and the development of the Yangtze Economic Belt, China will form intersecting north-south and west-east economic belts primarily along the coastline, the Yangtze River and major transport routes, as well as a framework of coordinated development between regions that ensures the free and orderly flow of factors of production, effective functional zoning, equitable access to basic public services, and development that is within the carrying capacity of the environment and natural resources. China will improve the master strategy for regional development which is to develop the western region, revitalize the northeast region, fuel the rise of the central region, and support the eastern region as it spearheads development of the country. China will also develop innovative policies and improve mechanisms for regional development, coordinate development between regions, and narrow the gaps in regional development. China will increase support to old revolutionary base areas, areas with concentrations of ethnic minorities, border areas, and poor areas.

China's strategic choices for balanced regional development towards national rejuvenation are as follows:

First, China will create a master strategy for regional development that is sound and effective, future-oriented, and suited to its actual conditions, based on comparative regional strengths, and covering economic, population, resource and infrastructure strategies.

Second, China will give full play to the regulatory role of the central government in balancing regional development, improve the system of laws and regulations in this regard, and ensure rational allocation of public resources, focusing on providing equitable access to public services.

Third, China will move faster to implement major regional projects. In pursuit of sustainable development, it will coordinate the development of population, resources, environment, the economy, society, politics, science, education and administrative resources between regions.

4. Balancing the Wealth Structure

Common prosperity is the defining feature of socialism with Chinese characteristics. In the endeavors to revitalize the Chinese nation, the most difficult task in socialist modernization is to achieve basic common prosperity for everyone. To enhance social etiquette and civility, it is essential to promote fairer national income distribution, and especially balance and fairness in national wealth structure. A fairer and more harmonious society with higher culture and ethics depends on progress in achieving fairness and justice in the structure and distribution of national income. In China's efforts to achieve national rejuvenation, balance in national income and wealth structure is of fundamental social, economic and political significance that affects the whole landscape.

There will be two possible tends in China's wealth structure: First, China will see a widening gap between the rich and the poor and greater imbalances in wealth structure, with a rapidly growing proportion of middle- and low-income groups and a slowly increasing proportion of middle- and high-income groups, meaning that the distribution pattern of national income will remain pyramid-shaped. Second, with a growing proportion of the middle-income group and rapid growth in the proportion of middle- and high-income groups, the gap between extreme high incomes and extreme low incomes will narrow considerably, and the distribution of national income will be a dynamic olive shape. The Gini coefficient of urban and rural households' comprehensive incomes will be no higher than 0.3; the Gini coefficient of household wealth will be no higher than 0.45.

To advance governance of the wealth gap towards national rejuvenation, it is critical for China to uphold the people-centered philosophy of development and ensure that all its people contribute to and gain from development towards common prosperity. China will fully implement the strategy of balanced wealth development through targeted poverty alleviation and targeted wealth management, and encourage its people to create wealth through innovation, hard work and legal means. China will expand the middle-income group, raise the income of middle- and low-income groups, impose income limits on the middle- and high-income groups, narrow the urban-rural income gap between regional industries, and eradicate extreme polarization of wealth. The main measures are to expand reform of the income distribution system, improve the social security system, and build a fairer social environment. China will work hard to narrow the widening income gap between urban and rural areas, between regions, between industries and between social groups, and strengthen the rule of law in promoting fairer income distribution.

Modernizing Social Security

Social security is a public welfare system through which a country ensures the livelihood of all its citizens. Improving social security is the basic goal of cultural and ethical progress. In its efforts to achieve national rejuvenation, China must advance social security in step with its people's demands, its social and economic development, and its political progress. China will develop a more efficient, higher quality and more sophisticated modern social security system.

1. Modernizing Social Security towards National Rejuvenation

Social security is commonly provided by modern countries. It consists of laws, policies and measures that ensure all members of society have access to subsistence allowances and basic healthcare should they lose the ability to work either temporarily or permanently. Economically, it provides a means of distribution and redistribution of national income, playing an important role in narrowing the income gap between members of society, eliminating poverty, improving living standards, and maintaining social stability. Legally, it is enforced by the country in accordance with relevant laws. Improving social security should be mandatory and socialized, aimed at promoting welfare and fairness.

China engages in providing social security in order to fulfill its responsibilities to all members of society, and to ensure that all citizens enjoy the basic rights stipulated by the Constitution. China's social security system mainly covers social insurance, social relief, social welfare, and social services. By the end of 2019, nearly 435 million people participated in the basic pension schemes for urban employees and about 533 million in those for rural and non-working urban residents; over 205 million people participated in unemployment insurance; nearly 1.03 billion people participated in basic medical insurance for rural and non-working urban residents; about 255 million people participated in work-related injury insurance; some 214 million people participated in maternity insurance.

A modern social security system should be built in step with social and economic development, which is commensurate with China's socialist system.

First, China will develop a modern security system based on the coordinated efforts of the government, market and society in which the government plays a fundamental role, supplemented by market and society.

Second, China will carry out comprehensive reform of the social security system. China will reform the social security system and the economic, income distribution, labor & employment, and fiscal & taxation systems in a more methodical and coordinated way. Meanwhile, China will improve the structure and mechanisms for responsibility-sharing to ensure that social security responsibilities are shared rationally and effectively between the central and local governments, and between government and market.

Third, China will improve the structure of social security governance and advance law-based social security. Measures will be taken to ensure law-based participation in social insurance and law-based implementation of social security schemes.

Fourth, China will increase the coverage and level of social security. The goal of benefitting all its people will be realized through institutional improvement.

Fifth, China will promote a fairer social security system. China will work to see that everyone has access to social security and that the policies are consistent. China will improve the basic pension schemes for urban employees and for rural and non-working urban residents, basic medical insurance for rural and non-working urban residents, unemployment insurance, work-related injury insurance, and maternity insurance. China will also improve the social assistance systems and the level of social welfare.

2. Modernizing Subsistence Allowances

Subsistence allowances are used to ensure a minimum standard of living for non-income and low-income residents, which is a basic prerequisite of civilization and humanity, representing a country's cultural and ethical level. The subsistence allowances system is the foundation of the national social security system, which determines the level and quality of the latter. According to statistics from the National Bureau of Statistics, in 2019, China granted subsistence allowances to 8.61 million urban residents and 34.56 million rural residents; 4.39 million rural residents living in extreme poverty received relief and assistance. Together these comprise 3.4% of the entire population.

To improve China's social security system, it is important to uphold humanitarian and socialist principles, and develop a modern subsistence allowances system that is commensurate with the strengths of China's socialist system and corresponds with the level of China's social and economic development. First, China should advance the subsistence allowances system which is in tandem with its social and economic development and fully reflects its social, economic and political progress and its sense of humanitarian responsibility. Second, China should improve certification of applicants for subsistence allowances.

The key to China's all-round effort to improve the subsistence allowances system is to address the problems of low allowances, allowance disparity, and inefficient oversight.

First, China needs to solve the problem of low allowances by developing an index system in step with its social and economic development. It will increase the allowance fundraising channels and raise their efficiency.

Second, China needs to narrow the huge gap in allowance levels. It will put in place a standard system that provides more equitable access to subsistence allowances in both urban and rural areas, to eliminate urban-rural allowance disparity.

Third, China needs to set more reasonable allowance standards. It will build mechanisms for raising subsistence allowances in tandem with growth and inflation, so that all people with economic difficulties keep pace with time and cultural progress.

Fourth, China needs to strengthen allowance oversight, and punish fake insurance, insurance fraud, and misappropriation of allowance funds. All-round efforts should be made to improve laws and regulations on managing subsistence allowances and ensure law-based fundraising, operations and payment.

3. Modernizing Poverty Governance

China is the world's most populous developing country, with a large poor population base, a heavy historical burden and complex causes of poverty. It is now working hard to eliminate material poverty and reduce cultural poverty. According to China's rural poverty standard in 2010, which is annual net income per capita RMB2,300 (calculated at 2010 constant prices), in 1978 the rural poor population was 770 million (97.5% of the population); in 2000 it was 462 million (49.8%); in 2019 it was 5.5 million (0.6%).

Based on the World Bank's poverty standards in US$ at the corresponding times: In 1949, with per capita GDP of only US$28, China had the highest ratio of poor population in the world (65% of the world total); in 1978, the corresponding figures were US$227 and 60%; in

2019, the figures were US\$10,276 and 10%. This made China the largest contributor to poverty reduction in the previous four decades since its reform and opening up in 1978, achieving universally acknowledged success in poverty governance.

To achieve national rejuvenation, China has set the following staged targets in poverty governance:

- By 2020, China will finish building a moderately prosperous society in all respects, and lift out of poverty all rural poor defined by Chinese standards;
- By 2035, China will realize basic socialist modernization, and lift out of poverty all extreme poor defined by the World Bank standards; and
- By 2050, China will complete building a great modern socialist country, and lift out of poverty all poor people defined by the World Bank standards, bringing itself to the level of developed countries in terms of relative poverty (low-income population).

China's strategies to modernize poverty governance include:

- prioritize improving public wellbeing, and advance the provision of law-based basic public services in a more standard and equitable way, ensuring that the gains of development benefit all its people;
- improve compulsory education, employment, social security, basic healthcare, housing, public health, public culture, and environmental protection;
- strengthen assistance to specific groups of people with special difficulties, and expand the scale of transfer payments to old revolutionary bases, areas with concentrations of ethnic minorities, border areas, and poverty-stricken areas; and

- speed up the reform of social undertakings, implement targeted policies for different individuals and regions to increase the impact of poverty alleviation, promote equitable access to basic public services in rural areas, and put in place a responsibility system for poverty alleviation.

China's measures to extend poverty governance are:

- build a poor population information network to strengthen dynamic tracing and monitoring of the real situation;
- bring Chinese poverty standards into line with the World Bank to fully reflect China's responsibilities in the international context;
- develop a national poverty alleviation system, including institutions, staff, capital, technology, and rewards & sanctions;
- leverage China's political and institutional strengths to beat poverty;
- advance major poverty alleviation projects, striving to lift all rural poor out of poverty by means of industrial development, alternative employment, population relocation, social security, educational & training programs, medical assistance, and work in eco-environmental conservation;
- encourage coordinated efforts of the government, market and society to improve the institutions and mechanisms for poverty reduction, and set up a trans-regional and trans-departmental poverty reduction system that involves public participation; and
- implement a responsibility system for officials involved in poverty alleviation, and develop an evaluation system for their performance.

Modernizing Social Fairness

To achieve higher degree of social fairness is one of the core aims of social progress. In the efforts to revitalize and modernize the Chinese nation, promoting comprehensive social fairness is a vital task. To make Chinese society fairer, it is essential to provide law-based public services in a more standard and equitable way, with priority given to fairness in education, healthcare, housing and employment.

1. More Equitable Access to Education

Problems of equal access to education in China mainly refer to inequitable opportunity between urban and rural areas, between different regions, and between different households, manifesting in lower educational attainment among rural children and children of migrant workers & low-income urban residents. To promote fairness in education, China will ensure equal access to quality public education resources, and apply standardization, the rule of law and IT. All efforts will be made to overcome the imbalances between urban and rural areas, between different regions and between different households, in terms of school facilities and education quality as well as educational polices, systems and mechanisms.

China will promote urban-rural education fairness in three key areas: First, it will improve legislation on equal access to standardized education for all areas, and define responsibilities, objectives, implementation requirements, rewards and sanctions. Second, it will define a time limit to address inadequacies in rural public education, by increasing inputs, improving quality, and directing more resources to the countryside. Efforts will be made to encourage more urban teachers to work in rural areas by rotating teachers and subsidizing their salaries. More will be done to improve the nutritional status of rural children. Third, it will give fairer access to education to migrant worker's children.

China will promote fairness in regional education in four key areas: First, it will compensate past shortcomings by increasing investment in education and educational resources in backward areas. Second, it will implement a plan to double teachers' wages in backward areas. Third, it will modernize education in central and western regions. Fourth, it will direct good-quality higher education resources to backward areas, and strengthen higher education in central and western regions.

China will make family education fairer. The key here is to make educational resources available to disadvantaged families. First, it will secure the provision of education, by supporting low-income families through redistribution, reducing poverty caused by lack of education, and reducing the number of dropouts due to poverty. Second, it will provide compensatory education to disadvantaged adult groups, and give better skills to less-educated parents. Third, it will encourage social organizations to provide educational services and guidance to disadvantaged families. Fourth, it will strengthen guidance and services for family education in central and western regions as well as rural areas of other regions, and for migrant workers. Fifth, it will help the public to develop a proper understanding of family education, and end absenteeism.

2. More Equitable Access to Healthcare Services

Healthcare is essential for safeguarding people's lives and health. A healthy population is a key mark of a prosperous nation and a strong country. Health is defined by the World Health Organization (WHO) as "a state of complete physical, mental and social wellbeing and not merely the absence of disease or infirmity".

Healthcare services aim to safeguard public health. Chinese hospitals numbered 9,293 in 1978, 16,318 in 2000, and 34,000 in 2019, growing at an average annual rate of 3.2% between 1979 and 2019. Chinese hospitals possessed 1.1 million beds in 1978, 2.2 million in 2000, and 8.9 million in 2019, registering an average annual growth rate of 4.5% between 1979 and 2019. Chinese licensed (assistant) doctors numbered about 1 million in 1978, 2.1 million in 2000, and 3.8 million in 2019, growing at an average annual rate of 3.3% between 2001 and 2019. China's healthcare expenditure totaled RMB11 billion in 1978, RMB458.7 billion in 2000, and RMB5.9 trillion in 2018, registering an average annual growth rate of 17% between 2001 and 2018.

To carry out the Healthy China initiative and ensure equitable access to quality healthcare services, China must commit to a people-centered approach, prioritize the development of public health, maintain basic not-for-profit healthcare, improve the national health policy, and ensure the delivery of comprehensive lifecycle health services for its people.

In implementing the Healthy China initiative, China will take the following measures:

- deepen reform of the medicine and healthcare system, and establish distinctively Chinese systems for providing basic healthcare;
- improve community-level healthcare services by providing more medical resources;
- improve public health services;
- support both traditional Chinese medicine (TCM) and Western medicine, and ensure the preservation and development of TCM;
- support the development of health-related industries to meet the people's diverse health needs; and
- improve population policies to promote balanced population growth.

China will promote healthcare equity in urban and rural areas. In 1980, there were 8.03 and 1.81 medical professionals per thousand people in urban and rural areas, respectively; in 2018, the figures were 10.91 and 4.63. In 1980, there were 3.22 and 0.76 licensed (assistant) doctors per thousand people in urban and rural areas, respectively; in 2018, the figures were 4.01 and 1.82. In 1980, there were 1.83 and 0.2 registered nurses per thousand people in urban and rural areas, respectively; in 2018, the figures were 5.08 and 1.8.

China will ensure more equitable access to healthcare services. In 1978, in national total healthcare expenditure, government expenditure accounted for 32.16%, social expenditure 47.41%, and out-of-pocket payments (OPP) 20.43%; in 2000, the figures were 15.47%, 25.55%, and 58.98%; in 2018, the figures were 27.74%, 43.66%, and 28.61%.

China will grow better at ensuring public healthcare services. In 1978, national healthcare expenditure totaled RMB11.02 billion, accounting for 3% of GDP, with per capita healthcare expenditure being RMB11.45; in 2000, national healthcare expenditure totaled RMB458.66 billion, accounting for 4.57% of GDP, with per capita healthcare expenditure being RMB361.88 (RMB812.95 for urban residents and RMB214.93 for rural residents); in 2018, national healthcare expenditure totaled RMB5.91 trillion, accounting for 6.57% of GDP, with per capita healthcare expenditure being RMB4,236.98.

China will ensure more equitable access to healthcare services. China will promote healthcare equity, develop a mandatory system of basic healthcare services, and improve the quality and level of healthcare equity in tandem with its social and economic development. China will narrow the gaps between urban and rural areas, between regions, and between households in basic healthcare services. China will put in place a diverse and multilevel healthcare system with universal coverage. This system ensures that everyone has access to basic healthcare services; its medical expenses are covered through diverse channels; and it is aimed at meeting the needs of different groups and protecting the right to health of all people in the country.

China will extend reform of the medicine and healthcare system, establish distinctive Chinese systems for providing basic healthcare, medical insurance and healthcare services, and develop a sound modern hospital management system. China will improve community-level healthcare services, and strengthen the ranks of general practitioners. China will stop hospitals from funding their operations with profits from overpriced drugs, and improve the system for medicine supply. China will emphasize prevention in extensive patriotic health campaigns, promote healthy and positive lifestyles, and prevent and control major diseases. China will initiate a food safety strategy to ensure that people feel secure about what they are putting on their plates. China will support both traditional Chinese medicine (TCM) and Western medicine, and ensure the preservation and development of TCM. China will ensure that its childbirth policy meshes with related social and economic policies, and carry out research on the population development strategy. As China responds proactively to population aging, it will adopt policies and foster a social environment in which senior citizens are respected and cared for and live happily in their later years. China will provide integrated elderly care and medical services, and accelerate old-age programs and industries.

3. More Equitable Access to Housing

Housing is a necessity of life. Fair housing is an important part of social fairness. Houses are for living in, not for speculation. Under this principle, China will put in place a housing system that ensures supply through multiple sources, provides housing support through multiple channels, and encourages both purchase and renting. This will allow China to meet the housing needs of all its people.

Since the market-based housing reform in 1997, owner-occupation has grown rapidly among urban residents, meaning that the real estate market now provides access to housing for most Chinese people. The market-based housing supply has rapidly increased homeownership among urban residents, and contributed to a consistent rise in real estate prices and the asset value of their housing. Chinese housing falls into three categories: famers' self-built housing, urban residents' private housing, and public housing.

China's guiding principles for ensuring more equitable access to housing are: First, China upholds the principle of fairness in basic housing supply. The government will clearly define its main responsibilities, and specify the level of government investment to meet the minimum housing needs of citizens. Second, China will adopt a system of classified management for basic housing and private housing, through which basic housing is managed by the government, and quality housing and private housing are negotiated by individuals, market and society. Third, China will develop a progressive tax system for real estate holders, so as to ensure more equitable access to housing by levying fair real estate taxes. Fourth, China will put in place an official residence system for senior civil servants. Fifth, China will establish a system for all citizens to gain an equitable share of profits from unitization of state-owned land, and improve the systems for ensuring fair gains from state-owned land between urban and rural areas and between different regions.

At present, China's focus in the real estate tax system is on the following key areas: First, China will ensure that real estate taxes are shared by the people and benefit most people. Second, China will implement an open housing system for civil servants. Third, China will implement the official residence system of principal officials. Fourth, China will institute incentive mechanisms to promote equitable use of real estate taxes. A tax sharing system will be established, through which real estate taxes collected by the central government will be used for transfer payments to residential construction nationwide, and those collected by local governments will be used for transfer payments to regional residential construction. By levying real estate tax, China will advance the sound and sustained development of the real estate industry, ensure more equitable access to housing, and prevent and control polarization between the rich and the poor in real estate ownership.

4. More Equitable Access to Employment

Employment is pivotal to people's wellbeing, a guarantee for family life, and a foundation of social stability. Employment is a global problem. China is the most populous country in the world with the largest number of workers. In 1978, there were 401 million employed people in China, accounting for 41.7% of the total population. Of these, 70.5% worked in the primary industry, 17.3% in the secondary industry, and 12.2% in the tertiary industry. This shows that China was then a developing agricultural country with a large agricultural labor force. In 2018, the number of employed people was 776 million, accounting for 55.6% of the national total. Of these, 26.1% worked in the primary industry, 27.6% in the secondary industry, and 46.3% in the tertiary industry. From 1979 to 2018, employment grew at an average annual rate of 1.7%. Employment in the primary, secondary and tertiary industries grew respectively at average annual rates of -0.8%, 2.9% and 5.1%. This means that China has upgraded from a developing agricultural country with large agricultural labor force to a developing industrial country with the non-agricultural labor force playing the principal role.

According to the World Bank Database, in 2018, among the world's leading economies: 1.4%, 19.4% and 79.1% of employed Americans were in the primary, secondary and tertiary industries, respectively; the figures in China were 26.8%, 28.6% and 44.6%; the figures in Japan were

3.4%, 24.5% and 72.1%; the figures in Germany were 1.3%, 27.1% and 71.6%; the figures in the UK were 1.1%, 18.1% and 80.7%; the figures in France were 2.6%, 20.3% and 77.1%; the figures in Italy were 3.8%, 25.8% and 70.4%; the figures in Brazil were 9.4%, 20.4% and 70.2%; the figures in Canada were 1.5%, 19.5% and 79%; the figures in the ROK were 4.7%, 25% and 70.3%; the figures in Russia were 5.8%, 26.9% and 67.2%; and the figures in South Africa were 5.2%, 23.2% and 71.6%.

At present, China is transitioning from the middle to the mid-late stage of industrialization. In the coming 30 years, hundreds of millions of people in the rural labor force will transfer to the secondary and tertiary industries, creating a major problem for social fairness in China's modernization drive.

To increase employment, meet the needs of employment, and improve the quality of employment, it is essential to promote fairness in employment, including equal opportunity and fair pay. Employment equity means that equal employment opportunities are provided under the same conditions, and there are no discriminatory employment barriers outside the law. Fair pay refers to equal pay for equal work and emphasizes equal respect to every worker. China should ensure that all workers have fair job opportunities and wages, and equitable access to working conditions and labor security, and should not lose their jobs for invalid reasons.

Fairer employment will focus on the following:

First, China will improve employability by assisting workers to enhance their skills, and correct structural imbalances between workers' abilities and the needs of the labor market. China will improve the mechanisms and structure of human resource allocation, the quality of employment, the labor force participation rate, and labor productivity, so as to integrate employment and the economy through the efficient allocation of human resources.

Second, China will strengthen institutional guarantees to ensure fairer employment, make recruitment and competitive employment more transparent, and put in place a sound employment system without discrimination. China will improve the institutions and mechanisms for promoting employment and business startups, and public employment services (PES) in urban and rural areas. China will prioritize equal job opportunities and protect rights and interests to improve the quality of employment, and increase youth employment targeting college graduates.

Third, China will encourage the tertiary industry with its huge capacity for providing employment, and see that economic growth and employment growth reinforce each other. China will integrate the development of human resources with employability improvement.

Fourth, China will advance technical education and training, improve the employability and career choices of workers, and reduce structural unemployment driven by lack of skills.

Fifth, China will implement financial policies that help increase employment, create a favorable environment for entrepreneurship and employment, and carry out a national action plan for employment promotion.

Modernizing Public Safety

Better social security is a minimal requirement of social progress, including efforts to ensure life, workplace, transport, information and public security. To achieve this, China will continue its people-centered philosophy of development, work hard to meet the needs of the times and its people, and modernize its social governance.

1. Strengthening Life Security

Life security refers to issues closely related to the people's daily life, including safe food, drugs, daily requirements, drinking water and air. With steady social and economic development, people's lives have improved. People are becoming more sensitive to and concerned about the safety issues related to their daily life. And life safety issues play an increasing role in the government's efforts to ensure and improve standards of living. A safer living environment is an important component of China's social governance towards national rejuvenation.

Life security will be strengthened by the following measures:

First, China will improve laws, regulations, emergency response, credibility of manufacturers, and IT application, and increase rewards and sanctions.

Second, China will put in place a comprehensive governance system. It will harness the enthusiasm of various forces, including citizens, consumers, operators, industry associations, social organizations and network media to monitor life security, focusing on clear channels for complaints. It will implement a reporting system and protect the legitimate rights and interests of informants, and it will support the work of social organizations, including industry and technology associations.

Third, China will improve safety responsibility mechanisms in the production, circulation and consumption of products. Enterprises are the main producers and operators; they therefore bear the primary responsibility for workplace safety and product safety. The government must put in place responsibility systems for producers and operators, and an accountability system to guarantee product quality and safety. The country will implement a management system in which product safety responsibilities motivate changes in production and operation, and develop a regulatory system covering the whole process from production to consumption.

Fourth, China will build mechanisms to enable oversight over life security through public opinion. The country will provide publicity, education and reporting on life security and relevant issues, creating a social environment focused on life security.

Fifth, China will encourage technological innovation to ensure life security, improving product safety and quality standards, using advanced technology to reduce pollution in the production process, strengthening product quality and authentication through regulation, and applying technological innovations to control pollution, identify counterfeits and raise public awareness.

Sixth, China will build responsibility systems for food safety and product quality, and protect the rights and interests of consumers.

2. Improving Workplace Safety

To ensure workplace safety, prevention and control measures must be taken to avoid accidents that cause injuries or property damage in all work activities, to safeguard normal production processes in accordance with safety regulations, to protect the safety and health of employees, and to prevent damage to equipment, facilities and the environment, thus making sure that all work progresses smoothly. Safety at work is directly related to personal and property security, and more generally to reform, development and social stability.

To strengthen workplace safety in all respects, China must have a responsibility system for safe activity, law-based governance, safety awareness, emergency response, and technological innovation.

First, China will put in place a stricter responsibility system to strengthen the main workplace safety responsibilities of enterprises, ensuring that they meet their responsibilities for supervision and management and achieve strict assessment and accountability.

Second, China will implement law-based governance of safe production. It will improve laws, regulations and standards, strengthen supervision and law enforcement, improve approval and licensing procedures, and increase the efficiency of supervision and law enforcement.

Third, China will increase social awareness of workplace safety, enhancing publicity on and training in workplace safety, and promoting workplace safety culture.

Fourth, China will improve its emergency response capacity, enhance the source control of occupational hazards, and minimize injuries, casualties and property damage and losses.

Fifth, China will strengthen technology guarantees for safety at work, promoting IT application, and using advanced technologies to monitor all workplace processes.

3. Promoting Information Security

Since humanity entered the information society, information security has become increasingly important, being vital to national, political, economic and personal security. Information security problems in China, covering politics, the economy, the military and culture, and involving state organs, public institutions, enterprises, households and individuals, have a direct bearing on overall national security.

The main points in China's all-round efforts to strengthen information security include:

First, China will resolutely safeguard its sovereignty in cyberspace. Based on the Constitution, other laws and regulations, China will manage information and online activities within its sovereignty, and ensure the safety of information facilities and resources, especially key information infrastructure.

Second, China will resolutely safeguard its information security and network security. In accordance with the law, it will prevent, stop and punish any use of the Internet to subvert the people's democratic dictatorship, and to endanger national security, including theft and disclosure of state secrets; it will take resolute action against cyber terrorism and illegal and criminal activities.

Third, China will fully advance cyberspace cultural progress, developing ideological and cultural fronts on the Internet, nurturing and practicing core socialist values, giving play to the guiding role of moral norms, and building a civilized and credible cyberspace.

Fourth, China will put in place a law-based information and cyberspace governance system to integrate administrative supervision, industry self-discipline, technical support, public scrutiny, and social education. It will encourage social organizations to participate in cyberspace governance, and promote network public welfare undertakings.

Fifth, China will develop infrastructure for information and network security, strengthening the development and application of cryptographic technology, the training of network professionals, and the protection of cyberspace.

Sixth, China will enhance international cooperation in safeguarding information security and cyberspace security, and encourage the evolution of the global Internet governance system.

4. Enhancing Public Security

Maintaining public security is the fundamental requirement for ensuring the safety of people's lives, property and work, and social stability and harmony. It is also fundamental to continuing the Peaceful China initiative, and establishing a social governance model based on collaboration, participation and common interests. Along with social progress and economic development, the Chinese people have expectations of a better life, and higher standards for building a peaceful China. They pay more attention to personal safety, and the government's progress in combating crimes and maintaining stability. They focus more on whether or not their legitimate rights and interests are safeguarded, law enforcement is strict, and the administration of justice is impartial.

China will take comprehensive measures to improve public security:

First, China will improve the institutions of social governance and improve the law-based social governance model under which Party committees exercise leadership, government assumes responsibility, non-governmental actors provide assistance, and the public participate. China will strengthen public participation and the rule of law in social governance, and make it smarter and more specialized.

Second, China will improve mechanisms for preventing and defusing social tension, and properly handle problems among the people.

Third, China will promote safe development, and raise public awareness that life matters most and that safety comes first. China will improve the public safety system and the responsibility system for workplace safety. China will take resolute measures to prevent serious and major accidents, and build up its capacity for disaster prevention, mitigation and relief.

Fourth, China will put in place complete, reliable and efficient technological systems for public safety and social governance, providing technological guarantees for sustained, steady and safe social and economic development .

China will strengthen the system for maintaining public security:

First, China will expand institutional channels for greater participation by third parties, including deputies to people's congresses, CPPCC members and lawyers.

Second, China will improve the crime prevention and control system, and protect people's personal rights, property rights and right to dignity. China will build a responsibility system under which officials at all levels will perform their due public security responsibilities in places within their jurisdiction while first-in-commands are in charge of public security.

Third, China will build an information-based system to evaluate the people's satisfaction with public security, and develop a set of high quality and efficient institutions to study feedback. China will shift the focus of social governance to the community level, and improve the quality, efficiency and effectiveness of social governance.

Chapter 6

Modernizing Environmental Governance towards National Rejuvenation

China's environmental improvement faces a green, circular and low-carbon challenge – It must meet the ever-growing material and cultural needs of 1.4 billion people in its land area of 9.6 million sq km; it must strike a balance between population, resources, and the eco-environment; it must assume obligations and responsibilities to future generations, the world, and the earth.

In promoting eco-environmental progress, China should focus on the Beautiful China initiative, implement the fundamental national policy of conserving resources and energy and protecting the environment, and create green ways of work and life driven by technological innovation and institutional incentives. To build a modern socialist country of environmental progress, China must ensure harmony between humanity and nature, strike a balance between economic growth and environmental protection, and coordinate social and environmental progress.

Modernizing Environmental Progress

The key to environmental progress is to raise the awareness of the need to pursue green development, green production, green lifestyles, green transport, and green consumption. China should prioritize environmental protection and resource conservation as a fundamental national policy in promoting economic, political, cultural and social progress, and implement the policy through high-quality technological innovation and high-efficiency institutional incentives.

1. Environmental & Ecological Progress

Human society is faced with environmental crises, mainly caused by humans since the Industrial Revolution (1760s-1840s). Especially since the 1950s, global industrialization and urbanization have boosted world population and economic growth, while creating unprecedented global resource and environmental problems. Sustainable development has become a pressing issue before humanity.

Lying in the mid latitudes of the east of the Eurasian continent, China is a continental country with a vast territory. It covers a land area of over 9.6 million sq km, accounting for 7.1% of the world total (134 million sq km). The distance from east to west is about 5,200 km (a four-hour time difference), from north to south 5,500 km, and the direct angle of the sun varies by more than 30°. In addition, China has about 4 million sq km of sea area, 18,000 km of coastline, and many islands and islets dotting its territorial waters. Its mountainous terrain, active tectonic faults, complex water temperature conditions, and continental warm climate have directly affected population growth, agricultural production, and the development of civilization over thousands of years. They continue to do so today.

In its drive towards national rejuvenation, as the largest and most populous developing country, China is promoting industrialization, urbanization, IT application, marketization and globalization on the largest scale in human history, thus facing unprecedented challenges, including resource depletion, environmental pollution and fragile ecology. In densely-populated areas with rapid industrialization and urbanization, problems concerning population, resources and the eco-environment are more prominent and more serious. The energy structure is dominated by fossil fuels; the industrial structure features high energy consumption and high pollution; energy utilization patterns are characterized by low efficiency and high emissions. All of this has caused serious ecological damage, air pollution and huge public health risks, creating pressure for emissions reductions, and generating problems with a high cost of restoration.

Harmonious coexistence between humanity and nature is a must. Any damage to nature is ultimately damage to humanity. Pursuing economic growth at the expense of natural resources and the environment in any country is one-sided, abnormal, and unstainable. China cannot follow the old path of extensive growth, pollution, and unsustainable development. Instead, China must pursue green and sustainable development featuring harmonious coexistence between humanity and nature.

2. Guidelines for Modernizing Environmental Governance

Guiding ideas for environmental progress are: China must implement the fundamental national policy of conserving resources and protecting the environment; China should act on the principles of prioritizing resource conservation and environmental protection and letting nature restore itself; China should focus on improving the symbiosis between humanity and nature and addressing prominent environmental problems, work to guarantee environmental security, improve the quality of the eco-environment, increase resource utilization efficiency, and develop a new pattern of modernization with humanity developing in harmony with nature.

Environmental progress towards national rejuvenation means:

- China must implement the fundamental national policy of resource conservation, and strike a balance between economic growth and resource conservation;
- China must promote green development, and develop a green mode of production and a green way of life;
- China must pursue low-carbon development, and build a low-carbon economy and a low-carbon society;
- China must promote circular development, and improve the efficiency in developing and utilizing resources;
- China must pursue sustainable development, and ensure intergenerational equity of human development; and
- China needs to put in place a sound evaluation system for environmental progress.

Developing a better understanding of environmental improvement. It is a must to integrate environmental progress into the whole process of social and economic development. From strategy to planning, from funds to technology, from leadership to rewards and penalties, China will advance environmental progress on all fronts. In terms of environmental awareness, China must uphold the philosophy of sound and green development, promote greater harmony between population, resources, environment and development, and resolve environmental problems through legal, economic, technological and administrative means.

Providing greater technological support for environmental progress. China should start by solving problems of resources and the environment. China will prioritize science and technology in environmental progress and governance, encourage technological innovation that supports green ways of work and life to the maximum extent, and implement quality standard systems for green products, including green food, green appliances and green transport.

Improving the institutional guarantee for environmental progress. Institutional enforcement is a fundamental guarantee for solving problems of resources and the environment, and for environmental progress. China follows the guiding principle that the system, rule of law and standards precede anything else in environmental governance. China needs to put in place a unified real-time online monitoring and early-warning system for environmental conditions. China will develop an accountability system, a compensation system and a third-party governance system to enhance environmental consciousness – The accountability system covers responsibility for production, consumption, transactions, and scrutiny; the compensation system includes industrial, regional, enterprise, social, individual and state compensation.

Enabling more effective enforcement of environmental protection. China will focus on building, implementing and supervising a unified, well-conceived and firm system of rewards and penalties concerning resources and the environment. Only by doing so can China safeguard the authority of environmental governance. Especially for prohibitions and transfer payments in promoting environmental progress, rewards and penalties in place and effective enforcement are key to preventing the system from becoming mere window-dressing. If the prohibition system fails to realize zero tolerance, governance will be heavily damaged and even entirely ineffective; if the transfer payment system is not implemented thoroughly, the regional environmental protection system will be inefficient and even fail completely.

Modernizing Resource Conservation

China is a country rich in resources, but less so in per-capita share of resources. In the face of this problem, China is promoting industrialization, urbanization, marketization and modernization on the largest scale in human history, causing severe pressure on the environment. China must implement the fundamental national policy of conserving resources in social and economic development, manage the conservation of resources through a combination of economic, administrative and law-based means, and work to achieve sustainable development in the utilization and protection of resources.

1. Modernizing the Resource Conservation System

Natural resources are natural elements that can be processed through human labor and productive activities into the means of production and subsistence, including land (arable land, grassland, grazing land and forest land), energy (coal, petroleum and natural gas), mineral resources (iron ore, copper ore, aluminum ore and phosphate rock), fresh water (surface water and groundwater), the atmosphere, and flora and fauna. Natural resources can be divided into renewable and non-renewable resources, and movable and non-movable resources.

Natural resources are an important part of national wealth. The green GDP accounting system of the World Bank divided national wealth into three categories (2006): natural capital, productive capital, and intangible capital. Natural capital consists of underground resources, timber resources, non-wood forest resources, nature reserves, arable land

and grazing land, which can be compared internationally by market value. The World Bank estimated that the gross wealth of world natural capital reached US$28.6 trillion in 2000. This wealth was spread over the six highest-ranked countries as follows: the US 14.5%, China 9.8%, Russia 8.8%, India 6.8%, Brazil 4%, and Canada 3.7%.

The characteristics of China's resources are low per-capita share, unbalanced distribution, inefficient use, and very low security. All these make it essential that China must focus on low consumption, low emissions and resource conservation, and pursue green, eco-friendly and sustainable development in its modernization drive.

China must speed up efforts to conserve resources. China should have the strictest possible institutions and legislation in place to improve resource management and conservation. China needs to apply a property right system for natural resources, a system of paid use of natural resources and an ecological compensation system nationwide, and develop a modern law-based resource conservation & management system.

A resource recycling system. China will put in place a sound statistical system of resource productivity. China needs to implement the extended producer responsibility (EPR) system, encouraging producers to ascertain their responsibilities of recycling waste products. A waste recycling system should be set up for planting and breeding industries to promote integrated and circular development. China will expedite the creation of a garbage classification system. China will make a technical directory for the circular economy, and implement the policies of government preferential procurement and discount loans.

A protection system for natural forests, grasslands, and wetlands. China will develop a full protection system for natural forests and improve the collective forest ownership system and the grassland contracting system. China will practice a grassland protection system, improve the mechanisms of compensation and rewards for grassland environmental protection, and carry out practices such as prohibition of grazing, temporary suspension of grazing, rotational grazing and forage-livestock balance. China will implement a full protection system for wetlands, and prohibit unauthorized expropriation of internationally important wetlands, nationally important wetlands and wetland nature reserves. China will designate the functions of various types of wetlands, make protection and utilization behaviors more procedure-based, and put in place mechanisms for restoring wetland.

A protection system for desertified land. China will improve the enclosing system, strengthen enclosing and management infrastructure, tighten desertification control, increase vegetation cover, rationally develop the sand industry, improve management & protection mechanisms focusing on purchase of service, and explore new mechanisms combining development with conservation.

A registration system for ownership affirmation of natural resource assets. China will make resource conservation more targeted, standardized, and law-based. China should uphold the principle that resources are owned by the public while property rights are prescribed by the law, in clearly defining the subjects of property rights of natural resource assets in all territorial space. China will unify the registration of ownership affirmation of natural resource assets in ecological space, including waters, forests, mountains, grasslands, wastelands and shoals, and draw a clear distinction between public ownership, collective ownership and government ownership. China should adopt a systematic and holistic approach to conserving aquatic ecosystems, and distinguish ownership, right of use and consumption of water resources.

A property right system for natural resources with clearly defined rights and responsibilities. China will put in place a compensated transfer system of all natural resource assets nationwide. China will improve the natural resource management system and agencies which act on behalf of the public to exercise the ownership rights concerning minerals, waters, forests, mountains, grasslands, wastelands, sea areas and shoals in a unified way. China will implement mechanisms in which central and local governments manage public-owned natural resources on behalf of the public, according to the different types of resources and different degrees of importance in ecosystems, the economy and national defense.

Sound and effective resource pricing mechanisms. China will set up a resource pricing mechanism that can reflect the scarcity of resources and meet the requirements of environmental progress. China will commit to integrating costs, benefits and ecological conservation in the development of cost evaluation mechanisms for exploiting and utilizing natural resources, and include the rights and interests of resource owners and environmental damage in the pricing mechanisms of natural resources and associated products. Sound and effective systems of land price and mineral price will be put in place too.

Sound and effective mechanisms for environmental compensation. China will strike a balance in environmental progress between different regions through environmental compensation, basin compensation, atmospheric compensation, and green transfer payments. China will develop sound and effective mechanisms to use environmental protection and restoration funds, and adopt a holistic approach to conserving mountains, rivers, forests, farmlands and lakes, to promote comprehensive improvement, protection and restoration of the river eco-environment. A sound and effective system will be put in place for environmental regeneration. China will implement the systems of regeneration of croplands, grasslands, forests, rivers and lakes, make plans for their regeneration, and adjust the use of cultivated land in areas with severe pollution and over-exploitation of groundwater.

Technologies for efficient resource recycling. To ensure resource supply safety and accelerate green transformation of resource-based industries, China will vigorously develop technologies for the efficient exploitation and economic use of water and mineral resources, and build a system of technologies for efficient use of resources that is commensurate with the country's social and economic development level, to provide powerful technological support for building a resource-conserving and eco-friendly society. Technologies for efficient use and recycling of resources cover efficient exploitation and use of water resources, green exploitation of coal resources, exploitation of oil & gas and unconventional oil & gas resources, clean exploitation and utilization of metal and nonmetal resources, and waste recycling.

2. Modernizing Energy Development and Governance

China is a big energy producer and consumer. Ensuring sustainable development in energy, the economy and the environment is a major strategic issue. China is rich in energy resources, but its per-capita share is relatively low. Resources are unevenly distributed. There are significant differences in availability of resources and energy consumption between different regions. Large-scale and long-distance north-south coal transportation, north-south oil transport, west-east gas transmission, and west-east electricity transmission form the basic characteristics of energy flow and the basic structure of energy transport in China.

Energy provides important material conditions for the survival and development of human society, and acts as a fundamental element of the economy, playing an important role in meeting the people's increasing needs for a better life. China's energy production was 628 million tons of standard coal in 1978, 1.39 billion tons in 2000, and 3.77 billion tons in 2018, growing at an average annual rate of 4.6% between 1979 and 2018. Total energy consumption was 571 million tons of standard coal in 1978, 1.47 billion tons in 2000, and 4.64 billion tons in 2018, increasing at an average annual rate of 5.4% between 1979 and 2018.

Major problems in China's energy production and consumption are massive consumption, unbalanced structure, inefficient utilization, and high pressure on emissions reduction. The main objective is to realize clean and low-carbon development. China will see that by 2030, the proportion between the consumption of coal, oil & gas, and non-fossil energy reaches 4: 3: 3, and that the country can safely tide over demand peaks through its capacity for independent innovation. By 2050, the proportion between the consumption of coal, oil & gas, and non-fossil energy will reach 3:3:4; a sustainable energy system will be in place, focusing on independent innovation; China's energy industries will be internationally competitive, and its capacity for technological innovation will reach international advanced levels.

According to relevant plans and research data, key indicators of China's energy transformation by 2050 are:

- Total energy (total energy consumption in standard coal) will be less than 5 billion tons in 2020, at most 6 billion tons in 2030, and less than 6 billion tons in 2050.
- Energy structure (the proportion of non-fossil energy in primary energy consumption) will reach 15% in 2020, 20% in 2030, and 50% in 2050.
- Energy efficiency (energy consumption per unit of GDP) will drop by 18.4% in 2015 compared with 2010 (0.71 ton of standard coal per RMB10,000), reduce by 15% in 2020 compared to 2015 (0.62 ton of standard coal per RMB10,000), reach the world average level of 2015 in 2030 (0.44 ton of standard coal per RMB10,000), and reach world advanced levels in 2050.
- Environmental protection on energy resources (carbon emissions per unit of GDP) will decrease by 18% in 2020 compared with

2015, reduce by 60 to 65% in 2030 compared with 2005, and reach world advanced levels in 2050.

China's strategies in energy development are: to uphold the principle of "resource conservation, clean & safe energy", to build a clean, efficient, safe and sustainable modern energy system, and to pursue green, low-carbon and innovation-driven development that prioritizes resource conservation and secures supply & demand. China should focus on improving energy efficiency; transform growth models, restructure the economy and accelerate technological progress as a fundamental policy; and put in place an energy- and resource-conserving industrial structure, growth models, consumption models, and institutions and mechanisms. China needs to develop an energy-saving industrial system and enforce an accountability & evaluation system to meet strict energy-saving goals. Mechanisms should be improved to promote energy-saving technologies and encourage the R&D of energy-saving technologies and products. China will further reform the energy system, improve the energy pricing mechanism, and amplify the role of fiscal and tax policies in facilitating energy conservation.

In energy development and governance, China aims to: first, safeguard national energy security, and see that energy supply is adapted to energy demand and meets social and economic needs; second, reduce damage from energy production and consumption to resources and the environment, especially the damage of air pollution to public health.

Below are the main tasks in China's energy development and governance:

- to build a green civilization and implement the fundamental national policy of energy conservation, and advocate a low-carbon and low energy consumption approach to life and work;
- to improve the energy structure and increase the production and

consumption of clean energy; and

- to promote technological innovation in energy, be at the forefront of international energy innovation, and publicize new technology and new products that use clean energy. China will ensure energy security and pursue sustainable development of energy through an energy revolution.

In energy development and governance, China focuses on:

- advancing an energy consumption revolution in all respects and inhibiting irrational energy consumption;
- promoting an energy supply revolution and building a multi-supply system;
- encouraging an energy technology revolution and energy technological progress;
- promoting institutional innovation concerning energy; and
- enhancing international energy cooperation and improving the level of energy security. Through the Belt and Road Initiative, China will strengthen international energy cooperation and connectivity, and adopt a holistic approach to capturing overseas energy markets and developing domestic energy resources.

Modernizing Environmental Governance

China's modernization is the largest industrialization and urbanization project in human history. It faces unprecedented resource and environmental problems. Air pollution, water pollution and environmental pollution are badly affecting sustainable social and economic development, standards of living, and quality of life. To realize national rejuvenation, China must modernize its environmental governance in all respects and build an environmentally-conscious civilization.

To achieve this, China will get all its citizens involved in improving the environment and address environmental issues at the root. China will continue the campaign to prevent and control air pollution to make its skies blue again. China will speed up prevention and control of water pollution, and take comprehensive measures to improve river basins and offshore areas. China will strengthen the control of soil pollution and the restoration of polluted soil, intensify the prevention and control of agricultural pollution from non-point sources, and take measures to improve rural living environments. China will improve the treatment of solid waste and garbage. China will enforce stricter pollutant discharge standards and see to it that polluters are held accountable. China will improve the systems for credit assessment based on environmental protection performance, for mandatory release of environmental information, and for imposing severe punishments on environmental violations. China will establish an environmental governance system in which the government takes the lead, enterprises assume main responsibility, and social organizations and the public also participate. China will get actively involved in global environmental governance and fulfill its commitments on emissions reduction.

1. Modernizing the Environmental Governance System

China's main tasks in modernizing the environmental governance system are:

- to standardize the environmental governance system;
- to strengthen the rule of law in environmental protection accountability;
- to provide rational compensation for environmental damage;

- to increase transparency in environmental governance;
- to institutionalize rural environmental governance; and
- to integrate national environmental governance.

China will standardize the environmental governance system. China will put in place a national system for environmental protection management through unified planning, with unified standards, based on unified environmental impact assessment (EIA), under unified monitoring, and backed by unified law enforcement. China will set up national agencies for unified environmental regulation and administrative law enforcement which are law-based and procedure-based.

China will strengthen the rule of law in environmental protection accountability. A national transfer payment system for green development, which is balanced and systematic, will be in place to implement strict and progressive payment, reward and punishment, targeting industries, enterprises, regions and departments with high emissions, high pollution and high energy consumption.

China will provide rational compensation for environmental damage. China will build a sound and effective environmental governance system to charge for and levy tax on high emissions and inflict punishment on high energy consumption. Special efforts will be made to develop a sound and effective transfer payment system to compensate pollution victims. China will put in place a modern, law-based and balanced environmental protection system to punish polluters and compensate victims.

China will increase transparency in environmental governance. China will publicize environmental information on atmosphere, water and land, with emphasis laid on pollutant discharging units and supervisory agencies. China will put in place sound mechanisms to publicize information on the EIA of construction projects, and develop a government media spokesperson system for the environment. China will better safeguard the people's right to access environmental information, promote public participation in environmental protection, and ensure the law-based and orderly exercise of the public right to scrutinize environmental matters. China will build an online reporting platform and a reporting award system for environmental protection, and improve the systems of reporting, hearing, reward and oversight through public opinion. China will work to see that the licensing system for pollutants discharge is more equitable, implement a unified licensing system for enterprise discharges that covers all stationary pollution sources, and prohibit unlicensed pollutant discharge or discharges that do not comply with the licensing requirements.

China will integrate national environmental governance. China will put in place management systems for environmental protection that strictly monitor the discharge of all pollutants; improve institutions and mechanisms for administrative law enforcement on integrated urban-rural environmental protection; integrate oversight in different fields, by different departments and at different levels in an orderly manner; develop unified modern agencies and systems for environmental law enforcement and regulation.

2. Modernizing Climate Governance

Climate change has direct impact on humanity's survival and development. It may cause ice melt, harvest failures, species extinction, rising sea levels, and other serious damage. Complex in climate conditions and fragile in the eco-environment, China is vulnerable to the adverse effects of climate change. Actively coping with climate change is of vital importance to protecting the security of the nation's economy, environment and food supply, and ultimately securing people's lives and property.[1]

---

[1] Laurence C. Smith: *The World in 2050: Four Forces Shaping Civilization's Northern Future*, Chin ed., translated by Liao Yuejuan, Zhejiang People's Publishing House, Hangzhou, 2016.

China's meteorology is complex and diverse, covering six climatic zones – tropical, subtropical, warm temperate, mid-temperate, cool temperate, and intense-cold. Influenced by topography and monsoon circulation, China has a tropical climate, a subtropical climate and a temperate monsoon climate, as well as a temperate continental climate, a plateau and mountain climate and an oceanic climate. From the southeast coast to the northwest inland, heat and humidity conditions are significantly different. With an alpine climate, the Tibetan Plateau is deficient in heat; the area to the east of the Tibetan Plateau features a continental monsoon climate, having rainfall and high temperature at the same time; the area to the north of the Tibetan Plateau features a dry climate with little rain. The proportions of arid and humid land areas are: humid area, 32%; semi-humid area, 15%; semi-arid area, 22%; and arid area, 31%. Overall, China has a low precipitation, with arid, semi-arid and semi-humid areas accounting for 68% of its total land area.

China is faced with the following difficulties in controlling air pollution:

First, the extensive work and life habits are hard to change fundamentally in the near future. The intensity of air pollutant emissions keeps growing in densely populated and industry-intensive areas, and China is under high environmental pressure to accomplish the mission of reaching peak emissions by 2030.

Second, the spatial range of atmospheric pollution follows the expanding areas of industrialization and urbanization and keeps enlarging. The regional synchronization feature of atmospheric pollution becomes increasingly obvious, bringing high concentration of pollutant emissions in mega urban agglomerations in the north, east, south and northeast.

Third, severe and extreme air pollution are yet to be effectively curbed, and in key regions the campaign to prevent and control air pollution to make the skies blue again remains a formidable task.

The main constraints hampering air pollution control are:

- an unbalanced industrial structure in which the proportion of sectors with high pollution and high energy consumption is large;
- an unbalanced energy structure, with prominent problems of coal-fired pollution and motor vehicle pollution;
- a difficulty in assigning the main responsibility for pollution in regions and enterprises with high pollution and high energy consumption;
- inadequate efforts of relevant departments in pollution control; and
- all-round, systematic, effective and timely pollution control to be improved.

Modernizing climate governance towards national rejuvenation is a major strategy in sustainable social and economic development. Top priority should be given to enhancing the consciousness of air pollution control. China will put in place effective systems and mechanisms to inform and educate the public on the need to protect the environment, to advocate green production, green life and green culture, and to develop a healthy, civilized and economical consumption model. China will integrate education on low-carbon ways of work and life and addressing climate change into the educational system, and popularize a clear understanding of low-carbon living. China will ensure that social organizations play an active role while the public and all sectors of society participate in actions to tackle climate change.

China will strengthen institutions in air pollution control. China will make all-round efforts to modernize the governance system with regard to the environment and climatic issues. China will improve the laws and regulations concerning air pollution control and climate change. China will put in place a sound supporting system for carbon trading, and strengthen carbon-trading authentication. China will improve tax and price policies for air pollution control, improve the government's green procurement policy, and improve green credit, investment and financing policies.

China will ascertain the main responsibilities for air pollution control. China will clearly define the implementation responsibilities and improve the evaluation mechanisms, strengthen the accountability system, and put in place a sound statistical accounting system. A system of incentives and punishments will be developed for the response to climate change, and the completion of tasks in this regard will be included into performance evaluation of governments at all levels as a key element.

China will pursue technological progress in air pollution control. Technological progress is the most effective way to tackle climate change. China will promote a green approach to work and life through techno-logical innovation. China will encourage technological innovation that can reduce emissions, thus controlling the formation and increment of pollution at the source. China will encourage technological innovation in pollutant recycling, so as to reduce the stock of pollutants. China will en-courage technological innovation in climate change prediction and early warning.

China will promote international cooperation on climate governance. China will contribute to an equitable international climate system, and fulfill the international obligations that correspond to its development stage, due responsibilities and actual capacity. China will develop multi-field and multilevel international cooperation networks, strengthen cooperation with international organizations and developed countries, improve mechanisms for South-South cooperation, and help developing countries to increase their capacity for action.

China will improve prediction, forecast and comprehensive early warning mechanisms, risk management mechanisms, climate disaster management, and the planning and use of flood control projects.

Modernizing the Protection of Ecological Diversity

Ecological diversity is the most direct expression of an environmentally-conscious civilization. To protect ecological diversity towards national rejuvenation, it is essential to set achievable goals, improve institutions and systems, strengthen protection capacity, and put in place performance evaluation and accountability systems for eco-environmental progress.

1. The Importance of Ecological Diversity

Biodiversity is a condition on which humanity relies for existence, and also the basis for sustainable social and economic development. Biodiversity provides food, fiber, wood, crude drugs and other industrial raw materials for humanity, and plays an important role in maintaining soil fertility, ensuring water quality and regulating climate.

Protecting biodiversity, especially endangered species, is of strategic importance to sound and sustainable development. Biodiversity on the earth is the result of natural evolution over several billion years. Biodiversity covers the diversity of species, genes and the ecology, in which the number of species measures the richness of biodiversity. In the past 500 million years, the earth has been through five mass extinctions, all caused by natural factors. In modern times, living things on the earth are faced with the sixth mass extinction, which is, however, the consequence of human activity. The speed of species extinction caused by humanity is faster than any time ever in history. The extinction rate of birds and mammals, for example, is 100 times or even 1,000 times that in an undisturbed natural environment.

Protecting biodiversity demands effective preservation of rare and endangered species. Research indicates that there are about 14 million species in the world, of which 1.7 million (including animals, plants and microorganisms) have been identified. Due to increasing human impact, many species are at serious risk. By the end of the 20th century, more than 1 million species had disappeared.

China's ecosystems are rich in biodiversity. China is among the 12 countries with the richest biodiversity in the world. China has diverse types of ecosystems, with higher plant species ranking third in the world and vertebrates accounting for 13.7% of the world total. China is one of the world's four biggest origins of genetic resources. With abundant genetic resources, China is the origin of important crops, including rice and soybeans, and the main origin of wild and cultivated fruit trees, ranking first in the world in this resource. It also abounds with livestock species. China is rich in vegetation types, including forest, shrub, grassland, meadow, desert and herbaceous swamp. With a low forest coverage rate, China has its forests mainly distributed in the south and the northeast, and its grasslands in the north and on the Qinghai-Tibet Plateau.

China has a vulnerable eco-environment. About 55% of the total land space comprises ecological vulnerable areas at medium-level or above. Within this figure, extremely vulnerable areas account for 9.7%, severely vulnerable areas 19.8%, and moderately vulnerable areas 25.5%. The vulnerable eco-environment has greatly limited China's levels of industrialization and urbanization. Striking a balance between biodiversity protection and regional economic development has always been a major challenge for China's sound and sustained social and economic development. As the cradle of the Chinese nation, the Yellow River basin used to be a homeland rich in biodiversity several thousand years ago, where there were countless trees, flowers and all kinds of wild animals.

China's massive industrialization, urbanization, marketization and globalization enable its social and economic modernization, and at the same time pose a huge threat to the habitations of many species. There-fore, China's ecosystems are facing more pressure; strains and conflicts between population, resources and the environment become more prom-inent; and the protection of the ecology and biodiversity becomes harder. Due to global climate change and China's vulnerable ecology, the country must vigorously protect its ecological diversity, and effectively address the problems of devastation of forests, shrinking of wetlands, drying up of rivers and lakes, soil erosion, grassland degradation, marine pollution, ecological vulnerability, and climatic, geological and marine disasters.

China's ecological diversity is mainly threatened by seven types of human activity:

- serious damage to the eco-environment, including forests, grasslands and wetlands;
- excessive hunting and use of wild species resources;
- rapid expansion of urban areas and industrial parks;
- introduction or invasion of alien species, destruction of the original ecosystem;
- environmentally-unfriendly tourism;
- soil, water and air pollution; and
- global climate change.

According to relevant research, 90% of China's total grasslands are suffering varying degrees of degradation or desertification; 40% of its important wetlands are facing the threat of degradation; 10% of its high-er plants and 21% of its vertebrates are under threat; some rare and en-dangered species are yet to be protected; and the loss of genetic resourc-es continues.

2. Modernizing the Protection of Ecological Diversity

To protect ecological diversity towards national rejuvenation, it is critical to establish the awareness of respecting nature, following its ways, and protecting it. When distributing social productive forces, pursuing urbanization and implementing major projects, China needs to thoroughly consider the carrying capacity of natural conditions, resources, the environment and the climate. All activities that blindly, ignorantly, savagely, purposefully and illegally damage the environment should be prohibited. Top priority must be given to protecting ecological diversity in the endeavor to build a beautiful China.

China must understand the significance of protecting ecological diversity, and develop a greater sense of responsibility, mission and urgency. China needs to strengthen education on protecting ecological diversity, foster and popularize a culture of ecological diversity, encourage a green way of life, and create a positive atmosphere. China's long-range goals of ecological governance towards national rejuvenation are:

- Degraded ecosystems have been fundamentally restored, and sound and stable ecosystems have taken shape;
- vulnerable ecosystems are subject to a higher degree of conservation;
- the area of desertified land decreases 80%;
- the rate of mountains returned to forestry reaches 40%;
- endangered species are under better protection, with ex situ conservation rate reaching 100% and in situ conservation rate 90%; and
- endangered species have recovered.

China's main measures include:

- enhancing the capacity of ecological diversity protection;
- strengthening in situ conservation of biodiversity and promoting

ex situ conservation as necessary;

- advancing sustainable exploitation and utilization of biological resources;
- improving the ability to confront biodiversity threats;
- raising public participation and awareness;
- strengthening international cooperation and exchanges; and
- creating a complete ecological redline system.

3. Modernizing the System of Ecological Diversity Protection

In biodiversity governance towards national rejuvenation, China should focus on: improving legal and policy systems for protecting biodiversity; putting in place information, data, monitoring and early warning systems for biodiversity conservation; promoting technological innovation projects on biodiversity conservation; and establishing a biodiversity conservation fund, jointly sponsored by the government and society.

China will set achievable goals for protecting biodiversity. China will put in place an operational and visual indicator system and evaluation methods for eco-environmental progress, and improve the evaluation system for social and economic development with three key indicators: resource consumption, environmental damage, and ecological benefits. Different methods of performance evaluation will be adopted for different regions with different roles to play. To strengthen the rule of law in the structural reform of eco-environmental progress, China will formulate and improve laws and regulations on:

- the property rights of natural resource assets;
- development and protection of territorial space;
- national parks;
- territorial planning;

- oceanic preservation;
- responses to climate change;
- cultivated land protection;
- water conservation & groundwater management;
- grassland protection;
- wetland protection;
- pollutant discharge permission; and
- compensation for ecological damage.

China will:

- improve incentive policies for conservation and sustainable development of biological resources;
- prepare balance sheets for natural resource assets;
- work out accounting methods for assets and liabilities of water resources, land resources, and forest resources;
- create physical accounting materials;
- clearly define classification standards and statistical specifications;
- evaluate natural resource assets on a regular basis; and
- refine mechanisms to monitor and provide early warnings concerning the carrying capacity of resources and the environment.

China will implement a lifelong accountability system for ecological and environmental damage. Principal persons responsible, relevant leadership and department heads will be held accountable, based on outgoing audit results of natural resource assets as well as ecological and environmental damage. China will create a national oversight system for environmental protection and enhance the protection of wild animals and plants.

Chapter 7

Modernizing International Governance towards National Rejuvenation

In today's world, accelerated globalization is creating a global village. Over the past millennia, human society has become ever more like a community of shared interests, risks and future. Modernizing China's international governance towards national rejuvenation makes demands of the country's development, international cooperation and human progress – China needs to promote international trade, investment and economic cooperation, as well as technological, educational and cultural development worldwide; China needs to purse fair competition, connectivity and win-win cooperation, through consultation, shared risks and joint governance.

A Global Community of Shared Future

Globalization, a global village and a global community of shared future are the most striking trends in the development of today's society. Facing these trends, whether different countries and nations win or lose, in joy or sorrow, or even suffering setbacks and failure only, the process of globalization and the creation of a global village will accelerate and improve.

1. Globalization & Its Opportunities and Challenges

From ancient Africa 70,000 years ago to the modern 21st century, humanity has moved from tribes to the world and from remote antiquity to the present – from nomadic civilization to agrarian civilization, industrial civilization, and information civilization. Society is becoming more and more intelligent, modernized and globalized, which is the basic law of its evolution.

Globalization is a worldwide historical process in which communication extends from within nations to between nations, and from regions to the world. The globalization of the economy and trade came first, followed by the globalization of science, technology, ideology, culture and system – global trade, economic cooperation, cultural exchanges, movement of personnel, and international consultations; international flow of people, goods, commodities, capital, and information. Globalization is connectivity and mutual assistance between all peoples, nations and regions in the world, and a process of forming a global village and a global community of shared future.

Humanity has experienced three major waves of globalization: The first lasted from 1870 to 1914, in which the proportion of world exports in total world output rose from 5% to 8.4% and international trade grew faster than the world economy, bringing large numbers of European immigrants to colonies. Later, World War I (1914-1918) and World War II (1939-1945) broke out, leading to the Great Depression (1929-1933) and the world crisis of capitalism. In 1950, world exports accounted for 5.5% of the world GDP.

During the second wave from 1950 to 1990, the growth rate of world trade substantially exceeded that of the economy. In 1990, world exports accounted for 13.5% of the world GDP. The US, Western Europe and Japan took a lead in the process of economic globalization while international agencies of the United Nations grew fast.

During the third wave from 1990 to the present, China, India, ASEAN and other developing countries and regions have joined the world, and economic globalization affects all countries and regions. In 2010, world exports accounted for 31% of the world GDP, and exports of developing countries made up 62% of the world total. It is estimated that world exports will account for more than 53% of the world GDP by 2030.

Population growth is the basis of globalization. American scholar Laurence C. Smith (1946-2017) believes that the four major factors — changes in the world's population, human demand for natural resources, the process of globalization, and global climate change — have shaped humanity's future. Rapid world population growth is the primary driving factor of globalization. Research suggests that there were only 1 million people on the earth 12,000 years ago, and the respective figures reached 1 billion in 1800, 2 billion in 1930, 3 billion in 1960, 4 billion in 1975, 5 billion in 1987, 6 billion in 1999, and 7 billion in 2011.

Research from the United Nations shows that the world population will rise to 9.2 billion by 2050. Regional differences and structural imbalances in the distribution of global population have created huge gaps in development, welfare, opportunity and culture, leading to unbalanced and insufficient development worldwide – the coexistence of extreme wealth and extreme poverty, and of peace and war.

Industrialization is the driving force behind globalization. To date there have been four industrial revolutions worldwide since 1750. During the First Industrial Revolution (1750-1850), the world's total population rose from 800 million to 1.1 billion, and its GDP rose from US$0.5 trillion to US$0.7 trillion, with the UK as the leading power, industry and agriculture as the leading industries, and the steam engine, cotton textiles, metalwork and porcelain as the leading technologies. In the Second Industrial Revolution (1850-1950), the world's total population rose from 1.1 billion to 2.5 billion, and its GDP rose from US$0.7 trillion to US$5.3 trillion, with the US, the UK and the USSR as the leading powers, industry, communications and transport as the leading industries, and various new products and consumer goods as the leading technologies. During the Third Industrial Revolution (1950-2000), the world's total population rose from 2.5 billion to 6.1 billion, and its GDP rose from US$5.3 trillion to US$36.7 trillion, with the US, Japan, Europe and the USSR as the leading powers, the information economy and the technology-based service sector as the leading industries, and ICT (information and communications technology) and nuclear technology as the leading technologies. In the Fourth Industrial Revolution (2000-2050), the world's total population will rise from 6.1 billion to 9.3 billion, and its GDP will rise from US$36.7 trillion to an immeasurable figure, with China, the US, the EU, Japan and India as the leading powers, the service sector, knowledge economy and green economy as the leading industries, and green energy, green technology, green building and green transport as the leading technologies.[1]

Humanity's globalization is a process of global competition in which each chases the others, following through competitive stages of following, catching up and exceeding. For different countries and regions, globalization means increasing interconnection and interdependence, as well as intensifying competition and rivalry, and even sharpening contradiction, conflict and struggle. The widespread impacts of globalization strike not only the economy, but spread to the fields of politics, culture, education and science & technology, as well as ways of life, thinking & ideas, and morals & ethics.

2. The Era of Global Village & Its Worldwide Impact

Globalization makes the human community an integral whole while the global village ties human future together. Globalization and the global village reinforce each other, and a global community of shared future is taking shape quickly. It is modern technology that reduces the spatial and temporal distances on the earth; it is human communication that builds a community of shared future. Canadian scholar Marshall McLuhan (1911-1980) coined the term "global village" in his book *Understanding Media: The Extensions of Man* (1967). The appearance of "global village" broke the traditional idea of space and time, making people more closely linked to the outside and even the entire world, and turning humanity into a more close-knit community of shared future.

Entering the era of the global village, global differentiation and restructuring of interests are speeding up. The accelerated process of differentiation, combination and adjustment of interest structures and relations worldwide continues to improve global resource allocation effi-

---

[1] Hu Angang & Yan Yilong: *China's National Conditions and Development*, Chin ed., China Renmin University Press, Beijing, 2016, p. 315.

ciency and creates enormous opportunities and broad space for human development. But at the same time it makes the worldwide problems of development opportunities, economic equity, humanitarianism and environmental protection more prominent, and has profound and extensive impacts on the world economy, politics, culture, ideology and values. Common problems worldwide are becoming increasingly severe, including more intense international competition, sharper international inequality and polarization, higher risks from international speculation, increased global crime, terrorism and environmental crises, and intensified liberalization and cultural conflicts.

Globalization will contribute to more human exchanges and cooperation in the era of the global village. Due to rapid developments in science, technology and transport, global economic and cultural exchanges are becoming more and more frequent. In the meantime, globalization in the era of the global village is more likely to generate new conflict and turmoil worldwide. Globalization brings win-win cooperation and mutual aid, and also leads to differentiation, contest and conflict. Competition and cooperation will continue to promote development across the globe while differentiation and conflict will make the world more turbulent. There is a long way to go for humanity to safeguard world peace and promote common development. On that journey all peoples will face:

- growing global economic challenges and financial risks;
- international trade imbalances and unbalanced global development;
- resource, environmental, ecological and climatic issues worldwide;
- international crime, drug, cult and violence problems;
- problems of international politics and regional turmoil;
- terrorism, hegemonism, nationalism and extremism issues; and
- an increase in both conventional and unconventional security threats and global challenges.

In the era of the global village, globalization will bring more structural changes to the world. Humanity will see unprecedented changes in the international community – open & conservative attitudes, independence & dependence, transcendence & depravity, security & risk, profit & loss, and progression & regression. If humanity fails to pursue peaceful coexistence and win-win cooperation, and if humanity cannot reduce the gap in benefit structure, ideological confrontation, and cultural and religious conflicts, nature will take revenge on humanity, and humanity will suffer more unrest and disasters due to its extreme selfishness, paranoia and arrogance. Moreover, if some irrational non-state actors – especially terrorist organizations – gain sufficient destructive power, nuclear weapons themselves will be able to destroy humanity. A global village means closer communication and cooperation, and is likely to cause a sharper rise and fall of great powers and worldwide turmoil. A global village enables the fittest nations and countries to run wild, and presents the less powerful with gloomier prospects.

In the era of the global village, modern history with the rise and fall of the Western powers as the principal axis is changing. From the 18th century, following the Industrial Revolution and colonial expansion, Western industrialized countries dominated human history for about 300 years. In the 21st century, profound changes are taking place in the global economic landscape; emerging markets and developing counties are on the rise; the balance of international forces is shifting towards the East and the South. In 2018, emerging markets and developing countries contributed 80% of the world's economic growth, accounting for about 40% of the global economy; the BRICS economies accounted for over 20% of the global economy. Of the BRICS, China contributed over 30% of the world's economic growth between 2012 and 2019, earning a greater say in the formulation of international rules in the global economic governance system.

Four trends in the future world are becoming increasingly apparent: First, the unipolar system with the US as the core is going to decline. Second, the Third Wave of Democratization will ebb away. Third, global capitalism will find itself in a predicament. Fourth, the Western-centric world will have less influence. According to Liang Henian, Canadian expert in urban and regional planning, it took about 130 years for Spain, France, the UK and the US each to seek hegemony in turn. Spain and France went to war for hegemony. In the future, humanity will strike a balance between the universal values of self-preservation and coexistence. Will traditional Chinese philosophy, including the golden mean of Confucianism, embrace these two universal values?[1]

3. Prospects for a Global Community of Shared Future

There is only one Earth and all of humanity lives in a single homeland. Globalization makes the world a global village, while the global village turns humanity into a global community of shared future. Humanity lives in the same global village where different countries, nations and cultures are linked to and dependent on each other; they cooperate with and contribute to one another at a level never seen before. Meanwhile, there are increasing risks of competition, contest, contradiction and conflict among them. The international community has increasingly emerged as a close-knit community of shared future.

Today, humanity lives in a world with different cultures, ethnic groups, skin colors, religions and social systems, and all peoples on the planet have become members of an intimate community of shared future. This has made different nations, countries, regions and organizations a body associated in questions of survival and future that are in-

---

[1] Liang Henian: *The Cultural DNA of Western Civilization*, Chin. ed., SDX Joint Publishing Company, Beijing, 2014, p. 483.

dependent of humanity's will – global trade & investment and economic cooperation; technological, educational and cultural exchanges; food, energy, and financial security; resources, the environment, and climate change; divergence, conflict, and war … On March 23, 2017, the "global community of shared future" was written into the resolution of the UN Human Rights Council for the first time, marking that this concept has become an important part of the international discourse on human rights.

Xi Jinping has pointed out: "There is only one Earth in the universe and we have only one homeland. Stephen Hawking has raised the idea of 'parallel universes', hoping to find another place in the universe where humanity could live. We do not know when his hope will come true. For now, Earth is still humanity's only home, so to care for and cherish it is our only option. There is a Latin motto inscribed in the dome of the Federal Palace of Switzerland which says 'Unus pro omnibus, omnes pro uno' (One for all, and all for one). We should not only think about our own generation, but also take responsibility for future generations."[1]

In his book, American historian David Christian (1946-) adopts a "big history" perspective to gaze at "universe & humanity". He surveys human history and points to the unpredictable "end of humanity": In 1969, by landing on the moon, human beings took the first, hesitant steps towards leaving their home planet. Humans now have the power to destroy themselves and to do much damage to the planet. The great complexity of the modern global community has created new forms of vulnerability and the fearsome prospect of a major collapse. What remains unclear, then, is whether the modern revolution will lead to the emergence of a new global system capable of relative ecological, economic and political

---

[1] Xi Jinping: "Work Together to Build a Community of Shared Future for Mankind – Speech at the United Nations Office at Geneva", accessed February 9, 2020, http://www.xinhuanet.com/english/2017-01/19/c_135994707.htm

stability, or whether the accelerating change of the modern era is the prelude to a sudden, sharp collapse. Perhaps the fundamental paradox of the modern revolution is that on the one hand human control over the biosphere has increased spectacularly; yet, on the other we have not yet shown that we can use that control in ways that are equitable and sustainable. Are we really in control of our astonishing creativity as a species?[1]

The global community of shared future demonstrates the broadest international political picture for human development. It calls on all countries and nations to consciously consider the reasonable concerns of other countries and nations while pursuing their own interests, and promote common development of all countries and nations while pursuing their own development. We should not give up on our dreams because the reality around us is too complicated; we should not stop pursuing our ideals because they seem out of our reach. All countries should stick together through thick and thin and act in concert with a sense of responsibility. According to the UN's Earth Charter (1992), "We are one human family and one Earth community with a common destiny. We must join together to bring forth a sustainable global society founded on respect for nature, universal human rights, economic justice, and a culture of peace."[2]

All peoples should work together to build a global community of shared future, and build an open, inclusive, clean and beautiful world that enjoys lasting peace, universal security and common prosperity. Politically, all peoples should respect each other, discuss issues as equals, resolutely reject the Cold War mentality and power politics, and take a new approach to developing state-to-state relations through communica-

---

[1] David Christian: *This Fleeting World: A Short History of Humanity*, Chin. ed., translated by Liang Wangrui, CITIC Press, Beijing, 2016, pp. 184-185.

[2] "The Earth Charter", accessed February 9, 2020, https://earthcharter.org/discover/the-earth-charter/

tion, not confrontation, and by means of partnerships, not alliances. In terms of security, all peoples should commit to settling disputes through dialogue and resolving differences through discussion, coordinate responses to traditional and non-traditional threats, and oppose terrorism in all its forms. Economically, all peoples should stick together through thick and thin, promote trade & investment liberalization and facilitation, and make economic globalization more open, inclusive and balanced so that its benefits are shared by all. Culturally, all peoples should respect the diversity of civilizations. In handling relations among civilizations, let us replace estrangement with exchange, clashes with mutual learning, and superiority with coexistence. Ecologically, all peoples should be good friends to the environment, cooperate to tackle climate change, and protect our planet for the sake of human survival.

China's Globalization towards National Rejuvenation

The Chinese people's endeavor to realize national rejuvenation is accompanied by the accelerated growth of globalization, the global village, and a global community of shared future. China must base its international governance on its time-honored history and culture, inspire its lasting ability to innovate, contribute Chinese wisdom, Chinese solutions and Chinese civilization, and advance the development of a global community of shared future to achieve shared growth through discussion and collaboration.

1. China's Development in Globalization

China, an ancient civilization, is located in eastern Eurasia, leaning against the vast continent and facing the mighty ocean. Its 5,000 years of development has not only benefited its own nation and people, but also impacted on other countries and regions. More than 2,000 years ago, China had already launched Europe-Asia economic and cultural exchanges and cooperation.

The land Silk Road, an overland trade route linking China's hinterland with Europe, took shape between the 2nd century BC and the 1st century BC. It was in use until the 16th century, serving as a main channel of economic, political and cultural exchanges between the East and the West. In 139 BC, Emperor Wu of the Han Dynasty (206 BC-AD 220) dispatched Zhang Qian to the Western Regions, opening up the Silk Road leading to the Western Regions – This route started from Western Han's capital Chang'an (today's Xi'an in Shaanxi Province), or Eastern Han's capital Luoyang (in today's Henan Province), arrived at Dunhuang (in today's Gansu Province) via the Hexi Corridor, passed through Central Asia, and reached Italy and other European countries.

The maritime Silk Road, a sea passage of trade and cultural exchanges between China and Southeast Asia and Europe, including the departure lines on the East China Sea and the South China Sea, took shape in the Qin (221-206 BC) and Han dynasties, developed during the Three Kingdoms Period (220-265) and the Sui Dynasty (581-618), flourished in the Tang (618-907) and Song (960-1279) dynasties, and changed in the Ming (1368-1644) and Qing (1644-1911) dynasties. It was the most ancient sea route. The major commodity it transported in the Sui and Tang dynasties was silk, hence the name "maritime Silk Road". This route was also used for porcelain transportation in the Song and Yuan (1279-1368) dynasties, thus called the "maritime Porcelain Road". Meanwhile, the main goods coming into China via the route were spices, giving it another name – the "maritime Spice Road".

Since the beginning of the British Industrial Revolution in 1750, humanity has entered an accelerated period of globalization. Following the outbreak of the First Opium War in 1840, China was reduced to a semi-colonial and semi-feudal society. In 1870, China's merchandise exports accounted for 2.5% of the world's total. By 1950 this figure had fallen to 1.7%. Deng Xiaoping pointed out that China remained isolated for more than 300 years from the middle of the Ming Dynasty to the Opium War, or for nearly 200 years counting from Emperor Kangxi's reign (1661-1722) of the Qing Dynasty. As a consequence, the country declined into poverty and ignorance.

Since the establishment of the PRC in 1949, China has experienced successes and setbacks in its efforts to go global. In 1950, China's imports and exports totaled US$1.1 billion – accounting for 0.9% of the world's total and ranking 28th globally – which was equal to 5.5% of American figure. In 1956, Mao Zedong put forward the strategic idea that China would catch up with and overtake the United States within 50 to 60 years. In 1978, Deng Xiaoping set the goal that China would realize socialist modernization by the middle of the 21st century, and its per capita GDP would reach the level of moderately developed countries. In 1978, China's imports and exports totaled US$20.64 billion – accounting for 0.8% of the world's total and ranking 29th globally – which equaled 6.4% of the American figure; the trade deficit stood at US$1.14 billion.

China's reform and opening up since 1978 has brought the longest period of economic growth in human history, the greatest industrialization, urbanization and modernization, and the most remarkable process of poverty alleviation. Due to reform and opening up, China has benefited the most from and contributed the most to globalization, and fostered an open economy in a comprehensive, multilevel and wide-ranging way. Between 1979 and 2019, China's total export-import volume grew at an average annual rate of 18.4%. In 2019, its goods imports and exports totaled US$4.6 trillion, accounting for about 12% of the world's total.

Since reform and opening up, China has met the basic living needs of its 1 billion-plus people and lifted over 900 million people out of poverty, which is a significant contribution to the global cause of human rights. China remains firm in pursuing an independent foreign policy of peace and in strengthening friendship and cooperation with other countries on the basis of the Five Principles of Peaceful Coexistence[1]. Between 1950 and 2016, China provided foreign countries with over RMB400 billion in aid. Between 2008 and 2019, China's contribution to global growth averaged more than 30% per annum. Between 2016 and 2021, China is expected to import US$8 trillion worth of goods, attract US$600 billion in foreign investment, and commit US$750 billion to outbound investment; it is also expected that Chinese tourists will make 700 million outbound visits. All this means more development opportunities for other countries.

China's achievements, experiences and path since reform and opening up is clearly quite different from Western models, and provides a fresh example for backward developing countries to learn from. The Chinese people keep to the path of socialism with Chinese characteristics and uphold the Five Principles of Peaceful Coexistence in handling international relations. Being an active participant in globalization, China has become the biggest beneficiary of and contributor to globalization, not through military expansion or colonial plunder, but through the hard work of its people and their efforts to uphold peace. China has been treating other countries as equals and pursuing win-win cooperation. China's most fundamental contribution to world civilization is that it pursues rapid development and national rejuvenation without following the old path of colonial expansion, or causing conflicts between major countries,

---

[1] The Five Principles of Peaceful Coexistence are: mutual respect for sovereignty and territorial integrity, mutual nonaggression, mutual noninterference in each other's internal affairs, equality and mutual benefit, and peaceful coexistence. – Tr.

or exporting revolution, violence, power politics or cultural imperialism. This is the most precious asset for humanity in the era of globalization.

2. China's Globalized Development Philosophy

Since ancient times, the Chinese have always held these beliefs dear: "All people under the heaven are of one family"; "all the people are my brothers and I share the life of all creatures"; and "all nations should live in harmony". China has always aspired to create a better world in which "a just cause is pursued for the common good". Countries may have differences and even encounter problems with each other, which is to be expected. But we should not forget that we all live under the same sky, share one and the same home planet, and belong to one and the same family. Peoples across the world should embrace each other with open arms, enhance mutual understanding, and seek common ground while setting aside differences. Together, we should endeavor to build a global community of shared future.[1]

In China's endeavor to realize national rejuvenation, all of the above ideas reflect the wishes and vision of contemporary Chinese on how to view the world, go global and shape the future. China will stay committed to building a world of lasting peace through dialogue and consultation; China will build a world of universal security for all through joint efforts; China will build a world of common prosperity through win-win cooperation; China will build an open and inclusive world through exchanges and mutual learning; and China will make the world clean and beautiful by pursuing green and low-carbon development.

—China remains firm in pursuing an independent foreign policy of

---

[1] Xi Jinping: "Working Together to Build a Better World – Keynote Address at the CPC in Dialogue with World Political Parties High-level Meeting", accessed February 10, 2020, http://www.bjreview.com/CHINA_INSIGHT/Special_Edition/201802/t20180212_800117836.html

peace. China respects the right of the people of every country to choose their own development path. China endeavors to uphold international fairness and justice, and oppose acts that impose one's will on others, or interfere in the internal affairs of others, or allow the strong to abuse the weak. China will never pursue development at the expense of others' interests, nor will China ever give up its legitimate rights and interests. No one should expect China to tolerate anything that undermines its interests. China pursues a national defense policy that is in nature defensive. China's development does not pose a threat to any other country. No matter what stage of development it reaches, China will never seek hegemony or engage in expansion.

—China has actively developed global partnerships and expanded the convergence of interests with other countries. China will promote coordination and cooperation with other major countries and work to build a framework for major country relations featuring overall stability and balanced development. China will expand its relations with its neighbors in accordance with the principles of amity, sincerity, mutual benefit and inclusiveness and the policy of forging friendship and partnership with its neighbors. Guided by the principles of sincerity, real results, affinity, good faith, and upholding justice while pursuing shared interests, China will work to strengthen solidarity and cooperation with other developing countries. China will strengthen exchanges and cooperation with the political parties and organizations of other countries, and encourage people's congresses, CPPCC committees, the military, local governments, and people's organizations to engage in exchanges with other countries.

—China adheres to the fundamental national policy of opening up and pursues development with its doors open wide. China will actively promote international cooperation through the Belt and Road Initiative. In doing so, China hopes to achieve policy, infrastructure, trade, financial and people-to-people connectivity and thus build a new platform for international cooperation to create new drivers of shared development. China will increase assistance to other developing countries, especially the least developed countries, and do its part to reduce the North-South development gap. China will support multilateral trade regimes and work to facilitate the establishment of free trade areas and build an open world economy.

—China follows the principle of achieving shared growth through discussion and collaboration in engaging in global governance. China stands for democracy in international relations and the equality of all countries, big or small, strong or weak, rich or poor. China supports the United Nations in playing an active role in international affairs, and supports the efforts of other developing countries to increase their representation and strengthen their voice in international affairs. China will continue to play its part as a major and responsible country, take an active part in reforming and developing the global governance system, and keep contributing Chinese wisdom and strength to global governance. The future of the world rests in the hands of the peoples of all countries; the future of humanity hinges on the choices they make. The Chinese are ready to work with the people of all other countries to build a global community of shared future and create a bright tomorrow for all of us.

3. Focuses of China's Global Strategy towards National Rejuvenation

To realize national rejuvenation, China will pursue opening up on all fronts. China will promote international cooperation through the Belt and Road Initiative; take an active part in reforming and developing the global governance system; continue to forge a new form of international relations featuring mutual respect, fairness, justice, and win-win cooperation; join hands with the people of other countries to build a global community of shared future; and build an open, inclusive, clean and beautiful world that enjoys lasting peace, universal security, and common prosperity.

Following the development strategy of opening up on all fronts. Opening up brings progress, while isolation leads to backwardness. Opening up is the only way to national development and prosperity. Promoting reform and development through opening up is a powerful instrument through which China can achieve continuing progress. To achieve national rejuvenation, China will continue to develop an open economy of higher standards, introduce foreign investment and foreign technology, and improve the institutions and mechanisms for opening up, thus providing new driving force for, injecting new energy into and opening new space for its economic development. China will follow a more proactive opening-up strategy; improve the open economy which is mutually beneficial, diversified, balanced, secure, and efficient; encourage coastal, inland and border areas to draw on each other's strengths in opening up; develop open areas that take the lead in global economic cooperation and competition; and establish pilot open areas that drive regional development. With a more open and inclusive mind and broader vision, China will devote serious energy to cultural exchanges with the rest of the world and make due contribution to the progress of human civilization through communication and mutual learning.

Implementing the Belt and Road Initiative. The Belt and Road Initiative is China's grandest strategy in its efforts to realize national rejuvenation and build a global community of shared future, greatly promoting its social and economic development and the establishing of a new model of relations with countries along the routes. Running through the Eurasian continent, the Belt and Road connects the Asia-Pacific economic circle in the east and joins the European economic circle in the west, benefiting more than 60 countries and 2.2 billion people along the routes. In the distant past, the land Silk Road and maritime Silk Road were major routes of trade and cultural exchanges, which linked China with Central Asia, Southeast Asia, South Asia, West Asia, East Africa and Europe. Focusing on development, cooperation and opening up, the Belt and Road Initiative aims to strengthen shared growth through discussion and collaboration on the basis of equality and mutual benefit, and pursues policy coordination, connectivity of infrastructure, unimpeded trade, financial integration and closer people-to-people ties with countries along the routes. The Belt and Road Initiative is open and cooperative, aiming to bring tremendous development opportunities to China and other countries along the routes. At present, more than 140 countries and over 80 international organizations support and are involved in this initiative. Important resolutions passed by the UN General Assembly and Security Council contain references to it. A number of international summits and forums on the theme of the Belt and Road Initiative have been held and become institutionalized platforms for promoting global development and cooperation in a new era. It has been proved that the Belt and Road Initiative helps develop major country diplomacy with Chinese characteristics and a global community of shared future.

Developing international relations on all fronts. Now, we live in a time of kaleidoscopic changes that make the world constantly different. As the trends of global multi-polarity, economic globalization, IT application and cultural diversity surge forward, humanity today is more ready than ever before to progress towards peace and development and to forge a new form of international relations featuring win-win cooperation. China is a major country in the world and will become a strong country in the future. Major countries have to shoulder their responsibilities, as do strong countries. To achieve national rejuvenation, China will develop major-country relations with the US, Russian and Europe, foster win-win cooperation with other developing countries, and deepen relations with its neighbors in accordance with the principles of amity, sincerity, mutual benefit and inclusiveness.

China will advance the reform and improvement of the international economic governance system, steer the global economic agenda, safeguard and strengthen multilateral trade regimes, and make the international economic order fairer, more just and based more on win-win cooperation, so as to jointly address global challenges. China will undertake its international responsibilities and obligations, support and participate in UN peacekeeping operations, enhance international cooperation to prevent nuclear proliferation, take part in the settlement of flashpoint and sensitive issues, and jointly safeguard the security of international channels. China will stay on the path of peaceful development and continue to pursue win-win cooperation. The one precondition in upholding peaceful development and advocating win-win cooperation is that China's national core interests must be resolutely safeguarded.

China's Global Governance Policies towards National Rejuvenation

Accompanying globalization, the global village and a global community of shared future, the needs for global governance are increasing. China goes global, and the world needs China. There has never been such an era as today in human history, in which countries are so interconnected and share a common future.

1. Guidelines for China's Participation in Global Governance towards National Rejuvenation

In today's world, all countries are interdependent and share a common future. To achieve national rejuvenation, China needs the world, and the world needs China. China will uphold the global principle of pursing development on an equal, peaceful, cooperative and open basis, foster a new type of international relations featuring mutually beneficial cooperation, and advance the building of a global community of shared future.

On the globalized aspects of China's national rejuvenation, Xi Jinping pointed out: The CPC is the largest political party in the world. Everything the Chinese Communists are doing is to better the lives of the Chinese people, renew the Chinese nation, and promote peace and development for humanity. China must run its own house well, which in itself is a contribution to the building of a global community of shared future. China must also see that its development will create more opportunities for the world. China will draw on its own experience to explore the evolution of human society, and share with other countries what it has learned. China does not want to "import" models from other countries, nor does it want to "export" the Chinese model, still less will it ask other countries to copy Chinese practice.[1]

—China will endeavor to build a world of universal security free from fear. We should foster new thinking on common, comprehensive, cooperative and sustainable security and create a security environment featuring fairness, justice, joint efforts and shared interests. We should jointly remove the root causes of war, reach out to those displaced by fighting, and protect women and children from the scourge of war so

---

[1] Xi Jinping: "Working Together to Build a Better World – Keynote Address at the CPC in Dialogue with World Political Parties High-level Meeting", accessed February 11, 2020, http://www.bjreview.com/CHINA_INSIGHT/Special_Edition/201802/t20180212_800117836.html

that peace will radiate across our land and shine on the lives of the people.

—China will endeavor to build a world of common prosperity free from poverty. We should work to deliver benefits to all, and promote win-win economic globalization that is more open, inclusive and balanced, thus creating conditions for the common development of all humanity. Doing so will enable us to pursue common prosperity for all countries, eradicate poverty and backwardness that plague people in many countries, and make sure that all our children are well taken care of. It will enable all countries to benefit from development and all peoples to lead decent lives.

—China will endeavor to build an open and inclusive world free from isolation. We should always bear in mind that the world is a colorful place and that civilizations are diverse; and we should see that different civilizations enrich each other and add to the beauty of our world. We should work together to bring down cultural barriers on the ground, reject prejudices that stand in the way of human interaction, and eliminate cultural bias that prevents people from engaging with one another. We should see that different civilizations coexist in harmony and that all people enjoy cultural nourishment.

—China will endeavor to build a green, clean and beautiful world. We should ensure harmony between humanity and nature, and cherish the environment as dearly as we cherish our own lives. We should revere nature, respect it, follow its ways, and protect it. We should protect the earth, our irreplaceable home, heal wounds inflicted on the ecosystem and environment, and build a harmonious and livable home for humanity. This will enable the natural ecosystem to recover and regenerate itself and everyone to live in a good environment with lucid waters and lush mountains.

Principles underlying China's support for economic globalization are:

First, China will continue to foster an open economy that benefits all. China will make economic globalization more open, inclusive and balanced so that it benefits different countries and people of different social groups.

Second, China will continue to pursue innovation-driven development and create new drivers of growth. China will seize the opportunities of technological and industrial revolution, the digital economy, the sharing economy, artificial intelligence and quantum science; transform the model of development; and nurture new growth areas.

Third, China will continue to enhance connectivity and achieve interconnected development. China will build a comprehensive, all-round and multi-tiered Asia-Pacific connectivity network, and boost the real economy through building connectivity.

Fourth, China will continue to make economic development more inclusive and deliver its benefits to the people. China will make inclusiveness and sharing a part of its development strategies; properly handle the relations between equity and efficiency, capital and labor, and technology and employment; manage the impact on employment of new technologies like artificial intelligence; improve systems and institutions to uphold efficiency and fairness; and safeguard social equity and justice. China will invest more in education, medical care, employment and other areas that are important to people's lives; address poverty and the widening gap between the rich and the poor; and deliver benefits to more people.[1]

2. Advancing Democracy in Global Governance

Democracy in international relations is a natural element of global-

---

[1] Xi Jinping: "Seizing the Opportunity of a Global Economy in Transition and Accelerating Development of the Asia-Pacific – Keynote Address at the APEC CEO Summit", accessed February 11, 2020, http://en.people.cn/n3/2017/1111/c90000-9291318.html

ization. It is a key and a precondition to building a harmonious world and to lasting peace, common development and cultural progress for humanity. Without democracy in international relations, world multipolarity and economic globalization will lose its way; fairness and justice will not prevail in the international community; and it will be difficult to realize peaceful development. Power politics and unilateralism go against the fundamental spirit of democracy in international relations, which advocates that all countries should discuss issues as equals, and address international issues and handle international affairs together.

Upholding the principle that all countries are equal. National equality is the basis for peaceful development and cultural progress. All countries in the world, irrespective of size, strength and wealth, are equal in national dignity. International affairs should be addressed by all countries, instead of being monopolized or manipulated by one or a few major countries. Uncivilized practices – the big abusing the small, the rich oppressing the poor, and the strong lording it over the weak – must end.

Respecting sovereignty and non-interference in internal affairs. These are the principles set forth in the UN Charter and the true essence of democracy in international relations. Every country's independence, sovereignty and right to choose its own social system and development path are sacred and inviolable, and they must be respected and safeguarded. Interference or infringement by any country in any way must end.

Respecting the diversity of civilizations. The diversity of civilizations is not only an objective fact, but also a factor that drives human progress. Every civilization, with its own strengths and weaknesses, should pursue inclusiveness, instead of exclusiveness or clashes. To respect the diversity of civilizations is to recognize and respect differences in history, culture, social system and development model between countries, allow the peaceful coexistence and harmonious competition of different systems and civilizations, and let the people and history make the final choices based on practice.

Ensuring cooperation and common development. Democracy in international relations includes democracy in international politics, the international economy, and international culture. The fundamental way to realize democracy in international relations is to promote cooperation and exchanges on politics, the economy, culture, ideology and values between countries, and jointly build a community of common development of civilizations for humanity.

Advancing democracy in international relations. There are several forms and ways to ensure democracy in international relations: democracy in international relations within the framework of the United Nations; democracy in cooperation and exchanges between countries advocated by major countries; democracy in international relations proposed by NGOs; and democracy in international relations put forward by international citizens, enterprises, and communities.

Fostering sound interactions between major countries. Russia is China's largest neighbor and an influential world power, and the two countries will consolidate and develop a comprehensive strategic partnership of coordination. The China-US relationship is one the most important bilateral relationships in the world, holding a special and important position in China's diplomatic plans. Europe is an important actor on the multipolar stage, acting as China's comprehensive strategic partner.

Giving play to the active role of developing countries, regional organizations, and non-state actors (NGOs and multinational corporations). China will improve relations with its neighbors. China will continue to forge friendships and partnerships with its neighbors, foster an amicable, secure and prosperous neighborhood environment, and implement the principles of amity, sincerity, mutual benefit and inclusiveness. Northeast Asia, Southeast Asia and Central Asia are the strategic focus of China's neighboring diplomacy; they cover many of China's overseas interests and important close contacts, and radiate a strong influence.

Advocating and practicing multilateralism. China will actively participate in multilateral affairs; attach great importance to the role of the United Nations; support the G20, Shanghai Cooperation Organization (SCO) and BRICS to play an active role; help the Conference on Interaction and Confidence Building Measures in Asia (CICA) to play a bigger role; firmly safeguard world peace; and continue to uphold the purposes and principles of the UN Charter and other generally accepted fundamental norms governing international relations.

Establishing a just and equitable world order. China will work to see that all countries, especially developing countries, are able to participate effectively in the international decision-making process. China will uphold the Five Principles of Peaceful Coexistence, the UN Charter and generally accepted norms of international laws, leading the world towards peace and security.

Participating in matters concerning the international governance by international organizations. To realize national rejuvenation, China will continue to be part of the international governance affairs of international organizations. This will include:

- active participation in the maintenance of world peace and security;
- active participation in global institutional design;
- active advancement of the implementation and oversight of global rules; and
- active participation in the governance of public issues of the international community, focusing on global governance in security, the eco-environment, economic & trade cooperation, transnational crime and protection of human rights.

3. Safeguarding China's Core Interests

National core interests refer to vital interests, matters of national survival that must not be given up or betrayed. These interests are the prerequisite and basis for the survival and development of a sovereign state. China's national core interests include state sovereignty, national security, territorial integrity, national reunification, stability of the political system established by the Constitution, overall social stability, and the need to ensure sustainable social and economic development. Xi Jinping has reaffirmed China's commitment to peaceful development. China does not covet other countries' rights and interests or look on with jealousy at their achievements, nor does it give up its legitimate rights and interests. Saber rattling cannot scare the Chinese people. They do not make trouble, but when it comes, they will not back away. China will not let any country force it to betray its core interests or undermine its sovereignty, security, and developmental interests.

To safeguard national core interests towards national rejuvenation, it is imperative to actively respond to international risks and challenges concerning land borders, territorial waters sovereignty, overseas investment and overseas Chinese, as well as those brought by separatist forces, hostile organizations and hostile ideologies.

First, China will actively develop a global united front to safeguard national core interests. The united front is one of the three keys to China's success and an important way to safeguard its national core interests.

Second, China will work hard to improve its ability to prevent and control international risks. International risks are the possible or probable damage or disaster caused by international events, including international economic, political and social risks and the risk of war. China will keep enhancing its ability to identify, assess, prevent and control international risks, and to act decisively when required.

Third, China will continue to improve its international competitiveness, covering economic, political, cultural, social, technological, military and diplomatic fields.

Fourth, China will actively support and join UN peacekeeping operations, strengthen cooperation on the international anti-terrorism campaign and nonproliferation, join forces with other countries in safeguarding the security of international channels, participate in the protection of global cybersecurity, and enhance foreign assistance and cooperation.

4. Modernizing the National Defense and the Armed Forces

National defense is the buttress of national security, and the military is the guardian of peaceful development. To achieve national rejuvenation, China must modernize its national defense and military capability; build world-class forces that meet the current and future needs of its national security and are commensurate with its international status; safeguard the security of its territory, sovereignty, development, and politics; and continue to modernize national defense and the military with Chinese characteristics, so as to provide the most reliable security guarantee for the country and the people.

Situated in the eastern part of Eurasia and on the western shore of the Pacific, China covers a total land area of around 9.6 million sq km and has territorial seas of about 3 million sq km. From south to north it stretches around 5,500 km, and from east to west around 5,200 km. China's land boundary stretches for over 22,000 km along Eastern Asia, and its marine boundary reaches about 18,000 km, penetrating deeply into Asia in the west and facing the Pacific in the southeast. China is therefore a densely populated country, interwoven with ethnic, religious and territorial conflicts, with a complicated geopolitical environment and many neighbors. It faces a complex security environment. To safeguard the security of its territorial land and sea and its core interests of national development and national rejuvenation, China needs to develop a comprehensive and multifunctional territorial defense capability that covers its vast territories. It must be commensurate with China's international status and able to contribute to maintaining world peace. In modernizing its national defense and the armed forces on the path towards national rejuvenation, China shoulders the heavy responsibility of building world-class forces, with a focus on how to enhance the creativity of national defense and the military.

Modernizing China's national defense and armed forces means integrating its comprehensive national strengths, consisting of science, technology, weaponry, equipment, materials, spirit, personnel and other elements. It is imperative to fully implement the military strategy for the new era, build a powerful and modernized army, navy, air force, rocket force and strategic support force, develop strong and efficient joint operations theater commands, create a modern combat system with distinctive Chinese characteristics, and transform the people's armed forces into world-class forces.

The missions are to resolutely uphold the leadership of the CPC and the socialist system with Chinese characteristics, to safeguard China's sovereignty, security and development interests, and to maintain regional and world peace. The main strategic tasks of China's armed forces are the following:

- to tackle a wide range of emergencies and military threats, and effectively safeguard the sovereignty and security of China's territorial land, air and sea;
- to safeguard the unification of the country;
- to safeguard China's security and interests in new domains;
- to safeguard the security of China's overseas interests;

- to maintain strategic deterrence and launch nuclear counterattacks;
- to participate in regional and international security cooperation and maintain regional and world peace;
- to strengthen operations against infiltration, separatism and terrorism so as to maintain China's political security and social stability; and
- to perform such tasks as emergency rescue and disaster relief, protection of rights and interests, guard duties, and support for social and economic development.

China's goal is to adapt to the trend of a new global military revolution and to national security needs. China will therefore upgrade its military capabilities to ensure that by the year 2020 basic mechanization has been achieved, IT application has made significant progress, and strategic capabilities have seen a big improvement. In step with this process, China will modernize the military across the board in terms of theory, organizational structure, service personnel, and weaponry. China will see that by 2035 the basic modernization of its national defense and armed forces is complete, and that by the mid-21st century its armed forces have been fully transformed into world-class forces. To achieve this, China will drive military practice with advanced theories, unleash the combat capacity and vigor of the armed forces by modernizing their organization, strengthen the military by relying on high-caliber personnel, and provide a strong material and technological support through an advanced weaponry and equipment system.

The following are China's strategic initiatives to modernize its national defense and armed forces in all respects:

First, to meet the political challenge, China will strengthen political work in the armed forces and integrate the leadership over the armed forces with efficient command. To this end, a new structure has been established with the Central Military Commission (CMC) exercising overall leadership, the theater commands responsible for military operations, and the services focusing on developing capabilities.

Second, to advance the rule of law in the armed forces, China will govern the military with strict discipline in every respect and build a well-conceived system to confine and supervise the use of power in the military.

Third, based on the need for a modernized elite fighting force, China will optimize the size, structure and composition of its troops to ensure higher quality and efficiency.

Fourth, to meet the requirements of modern military challenges, China will occupy the commanding heights in future military rivalries, give full play to innovation-driven development, and promote new ideas to drive the army's fighting capability.

Fifth, in accordance with the need for modern military personnel, China will better develop, manage and use its people, and put in place a modern system for personnel development, so as to bring about a situation where capable people emerge in large numbers and everyone can display his or her talents.

Sixth, based on the requirement for civil-military integration, China will make all-round efforts to implement the civil-military integration strategy, integrate economic growth and national defense, and put in place a comprehensive and highly-efficient network of civil-military integration.

Chapter 8

Modernizing Governance in the Lead Up to National Rejuvenation

The CPC is the core of leadership in China, governing the country for the people. The key to the governance of China is a well-functioning and well-disciplined Party.

It is critical to comprehensively improve the governance by the CPC, so that it can better assume its responsibilities and play its role as the core of leadership. The key to this is to comprehensively promote the Party's progress in political commitment, theoretical guidance, organizational improvement, improving conduct, enforcing discipline, and building institutions. Anti-corruption measures must be strengthened to improve the efficacy of Party development. The aim is to build the Party into a vibrant Marxist governing party which is always ready to answer the call of the times, enjoys the support of the people, has the courage to reform itself, and is able to withstand all tests.

Political Character and Strengths of the CPC

Founded in 1921, the CPC has gone through nearly 100 years of development and has become a Marxist political party unique in the world. One century of endeavor has shaped the unique political character of the CPC – firm in belief, well-organized, and with talent, vision and strategy. This is behind the success of the Party in the past 100 years in overcoming various difficulties and constantly forging ahead.

—The CPC possesses firm faith in the paramount importance of the people, and a spirit of selflessness and heroic sacrifice. From the founding of the CPC in 1921 to the birth of the PRC in 1949, more than 3.7 million revolutionists from the CPC whose names have been recorded sacrificed their lives for the causes of national independence, people's liberation, and national development; and the total number of CPC members who died for these causes is estimated at more than 21 million.

Since its founding, the CPC has never wavered in its political beliefs. Although the Party's specific tasks and requirements have evolved from the era of revolutionary wars (1921-1949) through the peaceful period of national reconstruction (1949-1978) and into the new era of reform and opening up (1978-), its fundamental political beliefs, purpose, goals and direction have never changed and will never change. As it advances the cause of national rejuvenation, the CPC remains true to its original aspiration and founding mission, and seeks happiness for the Chinese people. Its goal always corresponds to the people's aspirations for a better life and a brighter future.

—The CPC is well-organized: It works for the people; it has collective strength; and it has organizational support. To seek happiness for the people is the CPC's fundamental goal. The Party believes that a people-centered philosophy is key to its political thinking and that the people are the source of its strength. The CPC comes from the people, without whose support it would lose its foundation. Upholding its fundamental purpose of serving the people wholeheartedly and maintaining its close ties with the people must remain the fundamental requirements for strengthening and regulating political conduct within the Party.

Working for the people's wellbeing, the CPC is a strong Marxist political party organized towards a common goal, and a political force that is well-organized, well-disciplined and highly effective. The CPC has always emphasized centralization and unity of the entire Party, requiring its members to maintain political integrity, think in terms of the big picture, follow the leadership core, keep in alignment with the central Party leadership, and uphold the authority and the centralized, unified leadership of the Central Committee. The CPC's fundamental organizational line is doing everything for the people, relying on them, and following the principle of "from the people, to the people". The CPC emphasizes the collective wisdom and strength of the people, adheres to the people-centered approach known as the "mass line", and firmly believes that with collective strength the people can overcome any difficulty. Thus the Party unites all forces that can be combined for its mission.

The prosperity of the CPC's cause is primarily due to the growth in membership of the Party. The number of CPC members has grown from 53 in 1921 to 4.49 million in 1949 (0.83% of the total population), to 73.36 million in 1979 (5.5% of the total population), and to 90 million in 2019 (6.4% of the total population). The number is expected to reach 92 million when the Party celebrates its centenary in 2021. No matter the era or the country, such a large political organization is a powerful force for social change and development.

—The CPC has talent: a galaxy of talented people from every corner of the country. The CPC is a political party dedicated to the liberation of the working class, the happiness of the Chinese people, and the prosperity of the Chinese nation. Since its founding, the Party has been composed of Communists with knowledge, education and faith. Through the trials of revolution and war, and of victory and failure, they feared no death for their faith, and generations have constantly worked hard to serve the people. Such Communists form the main force of the CPC and its collective wisdom. History has proved that the inclusiveness of the CPC is key to the prosperity of its cause. Pooling into a mighty historical torrent, Party leaders, excellent Party members and the people together have toppled the old world and established a new China, and are building socialism with Chinese characteristics.

Advancing towards national rejuvenation, the CPC has united and led the Chinese people into a new era of socialism with Chinese characteristics. With new vision, it has built a deeper understanding of the rules that underlie governance by a Communist political party, the development of socialism, and the evolution of human society, and formed the Thought on Socialism with Chinese Characteristics for a New Era. It has enhanced the mission of remaining true to its original aspiration and constantly forging ahead. It has provided a stronger leadership, organizational support, and composite national strength for realizing the Chinese Dream of national rejuvenation.

To accomplish the historic mission, whether in times of weakness or strength, adversity or smooth sailing, the CPC has never forgotten its founding mission, nor wavered in pursuing it. It has united the people and led them in conquering countless challenges, making enormous sacrifices, meeting setbacks squarely, and courageously righting wrongs. Thus it has, time and again, overcome the seemingly insurmountable.

—The CPC has vision: It has confidence in the path it takes, its strategy, and its governance. From revolution to national development and to reform and opening up, from exploration to construction and to having confidence in its strategy, the CPC has overcome difficulties and obstacles, feared no risk, faced every challenge, and won victories one after another. The secret lies not only in the fact that the Party has firm faith, is well-organized and has talented people, but also in the Party's vision: a socialist path, a grand blueprint and strategic plans that are in line with China's reality and reflect the regularities of development.

Confidence in its chosen path fully reflects the CPC's political confidence. No other political party in the world today is so confident in its path ahead. The CPC has been able to build a modern socialist country that is prosperous, strong, democratic, culturally advanced, harmonious and beautiful from the ashes of a poor, weak and backward agrarian state. The key to its success is that the Party always represents the requirements for developing China's advanced productive forces, the orientation of China's advanced culture, and the fundamental interests of the overwhelming majority of the Chinese people, as it upholds and develops the path of socialism with Chinese characteristics.

Confidence in its strategy fully reflects the CPC's confidence in understanding. Based on the reality in different periods, the Party, guided by Marxism, has explored and answered major theoretical and practical questions, such as what kind of national rejuvenation to achieve and how to achieve it, and formulated and implemented a series of strategies such as building a socialist market economy, developing democracy and the rule of law, invigorating China through science and education, and making China a country strong in talent, enabling the Chinese nation to catch up with the times and usher in the bright future of national rejuvenation.

Confidence in its governance fully reflects the CPC's confidence in practice. Upholding Marxist historical materialism, the Party regards the fundamental interests of the people as its own interests, the fundamental will of the people as its own will, and the people's yearning for a better life as its abiding goal. The CPC upholds a historical, dialectical and thorough materialism. Based on its continuous exploration and understanding of the rules that underlie governance by a Communist political party, the development of socialism, and the evolution of human society, the CPC constantly improves and corrects its path of advancement, specific strategies, and ways and means of governance.

Mission of Party Development towards National Rejuvenation

Dedicated to the goal of national rejuvenation, the CPC shoulders a greater historical responsibility and faces even more serious risks and challenges. The Party must not forget why it started. It must continue to march forward, uphold its fundamental purpose and political nature, and modernize its governance in all respects.

China's century-long journey to national rejuvenation (1949-2049) means that it must achieve three major goals on the road of socialism with Chinese characteristics: overall eradication of poverty, completion of the building of a moderately prosperous society in all respects, and achieving modernization. After 30 years of hard work, China saw the basic needs of its people met in 1980; after 20 years of reform and opening up, it had basically achieved moderate prosperity in 2000; after 20 years of rapid development, a moderately prosperous society will be fully established in 2020. With another 30 years of unremitting effort, by 2050 China will have become a modern and strong socialist country which is prosperous, strong, democratic, culturally advanced, harmonious and beautiful, and will have realized national prosperity, rejuvenation and people's happiness, taking its place as a developed country in the world.

—Risks and challenges facing China towards national rejuvenation.

The CPC faces a complex governance environment. It is confronted with serious challenges and has arduous tasks to complete in Party development. In particular, as socialism with Chinese characteristics has entered a new era, the Party must take on a new image and accomplish new goals. To unite the people and lead them in realizing the Chinese Dream of national rejuvenation, the CPC must improve its leadership and make itself stronger.

Reform and opening up and the market economy promoted by the CPC have injected great vitality into the Party itself, but also exposed it to many new issues and new tests. The changes in the world, the country, society, the population, the government and the Party itself, especially the tests confronting the Party in governance, reform and opening up, the market economy and the external environment, as well as lack of drive, incompetence, disengagement from the people, inaction and corruption, have placed an even more daunting burden on the shoulders of the Party in modernizing its ideology, theory, membership and governance capacity, and given greater prominence to the issue of how to maintain the advanced nature of its members, especially leading Party officials.

In ideology and theory, the CPC faces the challenge that the general public and Party members are active in thinking and have diverse values. In a fundamental sense, the power and endurance of the appeal and influence of any political organization or political faction depend primarily on its ideology, theory, ideals and beliefs. To continue to lead 1.4 billion Chinese people to carry out socialist modernization and materialize its grand political blueprint and program, the Marxism-guided CPC must first meet the requirements of the times, adapt to social changes, further grasp the rules that underlie governance by a Communist political party, the development of socialism, and the evolution of human society, and propose a set of ideological and theoretical systems that are sound, effective and advancing with the times, so as to arm the whole Party, convince the people, win their support, and constantly improve its political credibility and appeal in governance.

Regarding its membership, the CPC faces a situation that its members are from various backgrounds and with different levels of qualities. They are from different professions and have different incomes, lifestyles and social status. All this makes it hard to determine their political ideology and motivation in joining the Party. In theory, the advanced political nature of its members is where the life and strength of any political party lie, and it is manifested in the specific political words and deeds and work performance of each Party member. In practice, the CPC's vitality, capability and leadership are mainly reflected in the sound quality of its members.

In improving its organization and rules, the CPC must answer two questions of fundamental importance: what qualified Party members should be like, and how Party officials should behave as expected. As a long-term governing party, the CPC possesses public resources, ruling status and power, which bring not only convenience in governance, but also difficulties in Party development. In practice, it becomes increasingly difficult to identify the political quality of Party members, especially their degree of ideological attainment in ideals and convictions. Some Party members have no faith though they belong to a Party organization. Some Party officials wield power but have no sense of Party principles or even integrity. This has caused unprecedented damage to the Party.

—Mission of Party development towards national rejuvenation. Development knows no boundary, nor does truth seeking or theoretical innovation. Today, China is closer to, more confident in, and more capable of making its goal of national rejuvenation a reality than ever before. In this context, the CPC must be prepared to work harder to comprehensively advance governance in the new era. The whole Party must strengthen its consciousness of the need to maintain political integrity, think in big-picture terms, follow the leadership core, and keep in alignment. All Party members must uphold the authority and the centralized, unified leadership of the Central Committee, be firm in implementing the Party's political line, abide by its political discipline and rules, and closely follow the Central Committee in terms of political stance, political orientation, political principle and political path.

In light of the changing realities at home and abroad and the historical tasks it undertakes, the CPC must strengthen itself as it advances towards national rejuvenation. The Party still has much to do to improve its leadership and governance capacity, its institutions, and the quality, competence and conduct of its members and officials. Only by ensuring effective self-supervision and strict self-governance and strengthening itself in the spirit of reform and innovation can the Party better withstand various tests and overcome various dangers.

To achieve national rejuvenation, the general requirements of the CPC for the new era are:

- upholding and strengthening the Party's overall leadership, and ensuring the Party's effective self-supervision and strict self-governance in every respect;
- strengthening the Party's long-term governance capacity, and preserving its forward-looking vision and its integrity;
- strengthening the Party's political commitment, and reaffirming its ideals, convictions and purpose;
- tapping into enthusiasm, initiative and creativity among the Party's rank and file;
- pursuing an integrated approach to raising its political awareness, strengthening its theoretical basis, improving its organizational structures, improving conduct, enforcing discipline, and enhancing institution building; and

- combating corruption so as to build a vibrant Marxist governing party that is always ready to answer the call of the times, enjoys the support of the people, has the courage to reform itself, and is able to withstand all tests.

In modernizing the governance of China for national rejuvenation, the fundamental requirement for the CPC is to uphold its political purpose of serving the people wholeheartedly. Except for the interests of the working class and the people, the CPC does not have its own special interests. At all times, the Party must put the interests of the people first, maintain the closest ties with them, function by the mandate of the people, empathize with their feelings, and work for their wellbeing. Party members must not lose their connection with the people or put themselves above the people. The CPC implements a people-oriented approach to work: It does everything in the interests of the people and relies on their strength, following the principle of "from the people, to the people", and translates its policies into the people's conscientious action. The CPC's greatest political strength is to keep close contact with the people, while its gravest danger is to become detached from the people. Improving Party conduct and maintaining close ties with the people determine the very survival of the Party.

Improving the CPC's governance capacity is at the core of modernizing the governance of China for national rejuvenation. The CPC must improve its approach to leadership and governance as well as its capability and performance in governance in accordance with the requirements of sound governance, democratic governance, law-based governance, secure governance, and institutionalized governance. The Party must ensure that its entire work meets the requirements of the times and the people's expectations. The Party must maintain and develop its advanced nature through good governance, to develop advanced productive forces, democracy, advanced culture, harmonious society and eco-environmental progress, and to realize the fundamental interests of the people and meet their ever-growing needs for a better life. The Party must ensure that it always stays at the forefront of the times and always maintains its vitality.

Strengthening the Party in the New Era

The CPC's Leadership means mainly political, ideological and organizational leadership. The Party must meet the requirements of reform, opening up and socialist modernization, persevere in sound, democratic and law-based governance, and strengthen and improve its leadership. Acting on the principle that the Party exercises overall leadership and coordinates the efforts of all involved, the Party must play the role as the core of leadership among all other organizations at the corresponding levels. It must concentrate on leading economic development, organize and coordinate all forces for this purpose, and promote all-around social and economic development. The Party must practice democratic and sound decision-making, formulate and implement correct lines, principles and policies, do its organizational, publicity and educational work well, and make sure that all its members play an exemplary and vanguard role.

1. Better Governance in the New Era

The CPC's political commitment is of fundamental importance. The primary task of strengthening the Party is to ensure that the whole Party obeys the Central Committee and upholds its authority and its centralized, unified leadership. All Party members must follow the Party's political line, observe its political discipline and rules, and align themselves with the Central Committee in terms of political stance, direction, principle and path.

The CPC must conduct its activities within the framework of the Constitution and other laws of the country. It must see to it that the legislative, judicial and administrative organs and the economic, cultural and people's organizations assume independent responsibility and work in unison. The Party must strengthen its leadership over trade unions, the Communist Youth League, women's federations and other people's organizations, and give full scope to their roles. The Party must adapt itself to the march of events and changing circumstances, improving its system and style of leadership and raising its governance capacity. Party members must work in close cooperation with people outside of the Party in the common endeavor to build socialism with Chinese characteristics.

The CPC is a political party that serves the people wholeheartedly. In the new era, it faces many severe challenges as well as many pressing issues within the Party, particularly corruption, disengagement from the people, formalities for formalities' sake and excessive bureaucracy on the part of some Party officials. The Party must make every effort to solve such problems. The whole Party must stay on full alert. As the saying goes, it takes good iron to make good tools. The CPC's responsibility is to work with all its members to ensure that the Party supervises its own conduct and runs itself with strict discipline, effectively solve major problems within the Party, improve its work style, and maintain close ties with the people. By so doing, the Party will surely remain a powerful leadership core in advancing socialism with Chinese characteristics.

Political corruption is the most serious corruption. It has two manifestations: One is to form interest groups and attempt to usurp Party and state power; the other is to form cliques, practice sectarianism, and engage in non-organizational activities, undermining the Party's centralized, unified leadership. Wang Qishan, former secretary of the CPC Central Commission for Discipline Inspection, pointed out: The Party must target interest groups in its effort to punish corruption, "take out tigers" and "swat flies", and prevent them from grabbing political power and changing the nature of the Party. The Party must eliminate factionalism and sectarianism in supervising intra-Party political activities so as to remove hidden political dangers. In the Party's anti-corruption campaigns, the 18th CPC Central Committee punished more than 440 officials with Party membership at and above the provincial/corps level, more than 8,900 at the department/bureau-level, and more than 63,000 at the county/division level, who have committed serious violations of state law and Party discipline. The Party's anti-corruption effort has been unprecedented and has achieved remarkable results. An overwhelming momentum has been formed and strengthened. In improving the self-supervision of the Party and the state, the CPC has broken the seemingly unescapable historical cycle of rise and fall.[1]

All Party members must hold the Constitution of the Communist Party of China in great reverence, act in strict accordance with the code of conduct for intra-Party political life under new circumstances, and make intra-Party activities more politically oriented, up-to-date, principled and effective. All Party members must guard against business dealings eroding intra-Party conduct, and foster a healthy political atmosphere of integrity within the Party. All Party members must improve and implement democratic centralism, and practice both democracy-based centralism and centralism-guided democracy. All Party members must foster values like loyalty, honesty, impartiality, adherence to fact and integrity, and guard against and oppose self-centered behavior, fragmentation, disregard of the rules, a silo mentality, sectarianism, factionalism and patronage. All Party members must resolutely oppose double-dealing

---

[1] Wang Qishan: "Usher in a New Era and Embark on a New Journey", *A Guide Book to the Report to the CPC's 19th National Congress*, Chin. ed., People's Publishing House, Beijing, 2017, p. 18.

and duplicity. All Party members, especially high-ranking officials, must strengthen their Party identity, political awareness, and political ability. All Party members must regard it as their fundamental political responsibility to be loyal to the Party, share its concerns, fulfill their obligations to it, and work for the people's wellbeing, and must forever preserve the political character of Communists.

2. Overall Leadership and Coordination

To always be the strong core leadership of Chinese socialism, the CPC must strengthen and improve its leadership, focusing on its fundamental political purpose of serving the public good and exercising power in the interests of the people. The Party must exercise overall leadership and coordinate the efforts of all involved; maintain its progressive nature and integrity; increase its creativity, cohesion, and effectiveness; and improve its performance in sound, democratic and law-based governance.

Formed and developed in practice, the CPC's status is a salient feature of the strengths of the Chinese socialist political system. The CPC Central Committee, the Political Bureau of the CPC Central Committee, and the Standing Committee of the Political Bureau of the CPC Central Committee constitute the Party's leadership core. The decisions and plans made by the Central Committee are implemented through the Party's organizational, publicity, united-front and political-and-legal-affairs departments, and through Party organizations in the people's congresses, the people's governments, the CPPCC committees, the people's courts, and the people's procuratorates. They are also implemented through Party organizations in public institutions and people's organizations. During these processes, and also thanks to a bottom-up information feedback system, the Party continuously improves and develops its decision-making capacity. This is the organizational and structural strength behind the

Party's survival and development over the past century. It is also what the Party must continue to strengthen and improve.

To strengthen and improve its leadership, the CPC should strengthen its long-term governance capacity and its advanced nature and integrity. The Party should constantly improve its ability to make overall plans and policies, advance reform, and lead social and economic development by improving its understanding of the rules of governance, development of socialism and evolution of human society. The Party should enhance its capacity to govern in an effective and democratic way and in accordance with the law, so that its governing strategy can be more effective, its governing system more complete, its governing methods more reasonable, and its governing status more consolidated. By strengthening its progressive nature and integrity in the new era, the Party should raise its ability to rectify, improve, reform and surpass itself, and increase its creativity, cohesiveness and effectiveness, so as to secure the victory of its cause.

To rejuvenate of the Chinese nation, the fundamental requirement for the CPC is to have strong political leadership, strong appeal to the people, strong organizing and mobilizing ability, and strong ability to renew itself. The Party should strengthen its core leadership status and core leadership ability as an overall goal, enhance both its political belief and its governance capacity, and promote Party development incorporating political education, theoretical guidance, organizational improvement, conduct supervision, discipline oversight, institution building and anti-corruption measures. Accordingly, the Party should properly address the following five deep-seated questions: how to improve its ability to lead by strengthening its political commitment, how to improve its guiding ability through theoretical development, how to increase its cohesiveness through organizational improvement, how to increase its credibility through conduct supervision, and how to improve its governance capacity through capacity enhancement.

3. Strengthening the Party

To lead the Chinese people to achieve the Two Centenary Goals and bring about the Chinese Dream of national rejuvenation, the CPC must remain fully committed to its basic guidelines, ensure its effective self-supervision and strict self-governance, strengthen its long-term governance capacity, and preserve its forward-looking vision and its integrity. It must advance Party building in the spirit of reform and innovation, and make all-round efforts to see its political commitment enhanced, its theory strengthened, its organizations consolidated, its conduct improved, and its discipline enforced. It must incorporate institution building into every aspect of Party building and step up efforts to combat corruption.

The CPC must uphold the principle that the Party serves the public good and exercises power in the interests of the people. The Party must carry forward its fine traditions and good conduct, constantly elevate its leadership and governance capacity, improve its ability to resist corruption and risks, and raise its capacity to rectify, improve, renew and surpass itself. The Party must expand its popular support for governance, strengthen its ability to innovate, power to unite, and energy to serve the people, and build itself into a learning, service-oriented and innovative Marxist governing party, so that it always remains ahead of the times and is always the strong core leadership in upholding and developing Chinese socialism.

To comprehensively advance Party building for national rejuvenation, the CPC must meet the following five basic requirements:

- adhere to its basic guidelines;
- continue to free its mind, seek truth from facts, keep up with the times, and apply a realistic and pragmatic approach;
- serve the people wholeheartedly;
- uphold democratic centralism; and

- exercise effective self-supervision and strict self-governance.

The CPC's strategic measures include:

- put strengthening its political commitment first;
- arm the whole Party with the Thought on Socialism with Chinese Characteristics for a New Era;
- train a contingent of competent and professional officials;
- strengthen primary-level Party organizations;
- work ceaselessly to improve Party conduct and enforce Party discipline;
- secure a sweeping victory in the fight against corruption;
- improve Party and state oversight systems; and
- strengthen every dimension of its ability for governance.

As Xi Jinping has pointed out, "A great cause calls for the leadership of a strong Party. As long as our Party keeps itself competent and strong, always remains true to the people's aspiration and works in concert with the people, we can and will navigate the great ship bearing the great dream of the Chinese people to conquer the waves and reach our destination."[1]

---

[1] Xi Jinping: *Secure a Decisive Victory in Building a Moderately Prosperous Society in All Respects and Strive for the Great Success of Socialism with Chinese Characteristics for a New Era*, Eng. ed., Foreign Languages Press, Beijing, 2017, p. 85.

Modernizing Governance Capacity in the New Era

From revolution to coming to power, from development to reform, from one victory to the next, the CPC shoulders a more and more important historical responsibility. This will ultimately be reflected in the Party's capacity for governance. As the CPC works hard to achieve national rejuvenation, its capacity building is mainly focused on the modernization of democratic governance, sound governance, law-based governance, secure governance, and institutionalized governance.

1. Modernizing Democratic Governance

Democratic governance is the primary task of the CPC in governing the country. To govern for the people, it must first govern the country democratically. This is the sole source of the Party's legitimacy.

The CPC should attend to the following:

- effectively organizing and leading the people to promote direct democracy in villages, communities, enterprises, public institutions, and government organs;
- effectively organizing and leading the people to implement indirect democracy at township, county, municipal, provincial and national levels, and to improve mechanisms for indirect democracy such as CPC congresses, people's congresses and CPPCC sessions;
- using direct and indirect democracy within the Party to effectively lead and demonstrate democracy at unit, urban & rural, and national levels, so that people's democracy not only becomes the basic political rights and interests of the Chinese people, but also a unique contribution from China to world political civilization; and

- reforming and improving the political systems and mechanisms that enable the people to be the masters of the country, including CPC congresses, people's congresses, CPPCC sessions, community-level direct democracy, regional ethnic autonomy and special administrative regions (SARs), so that Party members, Chinese citizens and ethnic groups have a stronger sense of fulfillment and pride in the people's democracy, and that China's good governance, people's republic and political progress win more and more respect and praise across the world.

The CPC must focus on strengthening and improving democratic centralism. Democratic centralism is the Party's fundamental organizational principle and an important institutional guarantee for sound intra-Party political life. Democratic centralism is a combination of democracy-based centralism and centralism-guided democracy. It is also the mass line applied in the Party's political activities. The CPC must fully expand intra-Party democracy, respect the principal position of Party members, safeguard their democratic rights, and give play to the initiative and creativity of Party organizations at all levels as well as their members. Centralism must be practiced correctly so as to ensure solidarity, unity and concerted action throughout the Party, and prompt and effective implementation of its decisions. In its internal political activities, the Party conducts criticism and self-criticism in the correct way, waging ideological debates on matters of principle, upholding truth and rectifying mistakes. Diligent efforts must be made to create a political situation in which there are both centralism and democracy, both discipline and freedom, both unity of will and personal ease of mind and liveliness.

Intra-Party democracy is the CPC's lifeline and provides an important foundation for active and healthy intra-Party political activities. The democratic principles and procedures laid out in the Constitution of the

Communist Party of China and other Party regulations must be followed regarding intra-Party decision-making, implementation and supervision. No Party organizations or individuals shall suppress or undermine intra-Party democracy. The principal position of Party members must be respected; their democratic rights must be safeguarded; and their rights to be informed, to participate, to vote, and to oversee Party affairs must be ensured. All Party members must be able to enjoy equal rights and perform their obligations as stipulated in the Party Constitution. The democratic relations of Party members as equal comrades must be up-held. No Party organizations or Party members shall infringe on the democratic rights of Party members. The Party must ensure that its members can participate in the discussion of the Party's internal affairs. It must broaden the channels for Party members to express their opinions, and create a political atmosphere for democratic discussion within the Party. Party members have the right to expose and report in a responsible manner any violation of state laws and Party discipline by any Party organization or Party member. Real-name reporting is advocated in this regard. Upholding the Party's collective leadership and combining collective leadership with individual responsibility based on division of work are important components of democratic centralism. No organizations or individuals are allowed to violate this system for any reason under any circumstances.

2. Modernizing Sound Governance

Sound governance is a requirement for the CPC to govern the country based on a sound understanding of objective rules. It requires both the ability to learn and the ability to apply. The ability to learn means that the Party should be able to learn from all human achievements and knowledge, and from all successful experience and inspiring lessons, and have a reserve of knowledge, experience, methods and cases that updates with the times, so as to provide effective intellectual guidance, theoretical support, experience reviews, and problem-solving methodologies. The ability to apply means that the Party should be able to apply the knowledge and methods it has learned and mastered to solve specific problems, advance specific work, and complete specific tasks. With this ability, the Party is expected to be credible, good at integrating theory and practice, and problem- and effect-oriented.

To achieve sound governance for national rejuvenation, Party organizations and Party officials at all levels are firstly expected to gain a good comprehension of objective rules, including the rules of governance by a communist political party, rules of building socialism, and rules of the development of human society, as well as knowledge of specific disciplines such as economics, politics, culture, sociology, ecology, military science and diplomacy. Secondly, they must acquire practical ability concerning policy making, strategic planning, and institutional operation in governance. In particular, the Party must improve the systems and mechanisms for collective and sound decision-making, and for community-level Party organizations and all Party members to effectively participate in governance, so as to improve its ability in sound governance through institutional strength and progress.

To revitalize the Chinese nation, the CPC is required to have self-confidence in its political system, belief and theory that helps it meet challenges and advance with the times. Moreover, the Party and its organizations and officials at all levels must have practical ability in strategic planning, design, guidance and operations.

Anticipating, managing and controlling strategic risks are extremely important aspects of strategic implementation. The more important a strategic issue is, the greater risks it contains, and the greater uncertainties it may bring about. Party officials at all levels, especially senior ones, must work hard to master the ability to anticipate, manage and control risks. Those who devise, organize and implement strategies must be able to analyze and estimate various uncertainties and potential crises, identify major governance risks and security challenges, and formulate feasible and systematic solutions for risk mitigation and control.

3. Modernizing Law-Based Governance

Law-based governance is the key to the rule of law. Safeguarding the authority, the dignity and the implementation of the Constitution and other laws means safeguarding the common will of the CPC and the people. Working for national rejuvenation, the Party must comprehensively improve its ability in law-based governance. This requires the CPC to govern the country and discipline itself in accordance with state laws & regulations and Party discipline.

In modernizing law-based governance, the CPC needs to do the following:

- comprehensively improving Party organizations' ability and performance to govern the country in accordance with the Constitution and other laws, so that the Party's views can be turned into the will of the state through legal procedures;

- comprehensively improving Party organizations' ability and performance to govern and discipline the Party in accordance with its internal regulations, and make economic, political, cultural and social life in the country more law- and norm-based; and

- comprehensively improving Party officials' awareness of and competence in law-based governance, so that they can take the lead in safeguarding the authority of the Constitution and other laws, scrutinize and support state institutions and guarantee that they exercise their powers in accordance with the law, and facilitate punishment of violations of state laws and Party discipline, to promote the rule of law in China in all respects.

The CPC will comprehensively build a leadership system for law-based governance. For this purpose, the Party will improve the systems and mechanisms for its leadership in law-based governance, and improve the mechanisms and procedures for its correct policy- and decision-making for the rule of law. The Party will strengthen the its unified leadership, planning and coordination for advancing the rule of law. The Party will improve the mechanism for Party committees' law-based decision-making, give play to the respective strengths of policies and laws, and ensure consistency between Party policies and state laws. Party organizations in the people's congresses, the people's governments, the CP-PCC committees, the people's courts and the people's procuratorates at all levels shall lead and supervise these units' exemplary compliance with the Constitution and other laws, and investigate and punish any breaches in law enforcement and abuse of power. The commissions for political and legal affairs of Party committees at all levels must uphold the correct political direction, coordinate the functions of all parties, coordinate political and legal work, build professional teams for political and legal affairs, supervise duty performance in accordance with the law, and create a fair judicial environment. They must take the lead in handling affairs in accordance with the law, and ensure the correct and unified implementation of the Constitution and other laws.

4. Modernizing Secure Governance

National security is an important cornerstone of national stability, and maintaining national security is in the fundamental interests of all Chinese people. China takes a holistic approach to national security. The CPC must ensure both development and security and always be ready to protect against potential dangers in time of peace. This is a major principle for the Party to govern the country. The CPC must put national interests first, protect the people's security as its purpose, and safeguard political security as a fundamental task. It must ensure both internal and external security, homeland and public security, traditional and non-traditional security, and China's own security and the shared security of the international community. The Party will improve the systems and institutions for national security to safeguard China's sovereignty, security and development interests.

Security is the foundation of development, and the foundation of the governance of China by the CPC. As the Party works to realize national rejuvenation, modernizing its ability in secure governance is of fundamental significance to safeguarding national security, the people's democracy and the socialist system with Chinese characteristics, protecting the fundamental interests of the people and the state, and ensuring the smooth progress of reform, opening up and socialist modernization.

National security means that state power, sovereignty, unity, territorial integrity, people's wellbeing, sustainable social and economic development, and other important national interests face no danger and no internal or external threats, now as well as in the future. In contemporary times, national security covers 10 fields: national security, territorial security, sovereign security, political security, military security, economic security, cultural security, technological security, ecological security, and information security. The core of these is national security.

As China strides forward to realize national rejuvenation, security is taking on a broader meaning. In the new era, both internal and external factors are more complicated than at any previous time in history. To ensure that the people live and work in peace and contentment, national security is a top priority. The CPC must never forget danger in time of peace, and never forget to guard against chaos when everything is in order. National security is the most important cornerstone of China's development and the most fundamental guarantee for the Chinese people's wellbeing. National stability and a peaceful life is their most basic and most common aspiration.

China must uphold the CPC's leadership over national security and build a national security system which is centralized, integrated, highly efficient, and authoritative.

To modernize the national security system, the CPC should strengthen its leadership over national security and build a holistic system for national security. The Party should establish a national security crisis management system that is under unified leadership, coordinated, orderly, and efficient. The Party should establish a personnel management system for national security institutions and an information reporting and release mechanism for national security crises.

In modernizing security governance, the CPC needs to do the following:

- improve the integrated system for maintenance of law and order, strengthen its overall social governance capacity, and identify and address problems and disputes at their source;
- strengthen industrial safety in such key fields as transport, fire prevention and production of hazardous chemicals, guarding against any serious accidents;
- consolidate the lines of defense for cybersecurity and protect key information infrastructure;
- proactively create a favorable external security environment and join the international community in strengthening cooperation for global security;
- enhance its capacity to provide the materials, technologies, equipment, expertise, legal guarantees and mechanisms required for safeguarding national security;

- rigorously protect against, and take resolute measures to combat, all acts of infiltration, subversion and sabotage, as well as violent & terrorist activities, ethnic separatist activities and religious extremist activities; and
- raise awareness of national security within and outside the Party, and create a strong synergy of the whole society to safeguard national security.

5. Modernizing Institutionalized Governance

A sound system is the foundation of good governance, and building systems is the foundation of the CPC's rule of the country. As Deng Xiaoping pointed out, the problems in China's systems are more fundamental, widespread and long-lasting, and have a greater effect on the overall interests of the country. In order to govern itself with strict discipline, the Party must have a strong system. Raising political awareness and building institutions should go hand in hand. Stronger institutional constraints must be in place at all levels, and so must more institutional oversight over the Party, over any exercise of authority, and over officials.

Improving the CPC's ability to develop and govern itself with rules and regulations, and its ability to govern the country with well-designed institutions are priorities. First, the Party should enhance its understanding of institution-based governance. Second, the Party should strengthen its internal rules and regulations. Third, the Party should strengthen its capacity to establish institutions. Fourth, the Party should strengthen its capacity to fight corruption in accordance with the law and institutional checks.

Promoting political integrity and combating corruption are important tasks for enforcing a code of conduct for intra-Party political life. At its sixth plenary session held in 2016, the 18th CPC Central Committee pointed out: "We must build up Party members' and officials' psychological defenses against corruption and vice, and strive to build a system and mechanism under which officials do not dare to be, are not able to be, and do not want to be corrupt. Officials at all levels are public servants of the people and are granted no special privilege. Officials, especially senior ones, must take the lead in practicing the core values of socialism, in stressing self-cultivation, morality and honesty, and in forming a sense of honor and disgrace. We must ensure that all cases of corruption are investigated and prosecuted, and that all instances of graft are rectified. We will continue to see that there are no no-go zones, no ground is left unturned, and no tolerance is shown for corruption, leaving no place to hide for corrupt officials within the Party. We must oppose and overcome formalism, bureaucratism, hedonism and extravagance, and form a strict long-term mechanism in this regard. We must improve Party conduct, uphold integrity and combat corruption, and ensure that Party committees fulfill their principal responsibility in improving Party conduct and upholding integrity, and that Party disciplinary commissions at all levels are tasked with conducting oversight and enforcing accountability."

6. Modernizing Governance Capacity

Leading a socialist country with a 1.4 billion population, the CPC must have both firm political beliefs and high competence. Xi Jinping has pointed out: "On our new journey, we are unlikely to walk on a flat road all the way. We will face many major challenges, major risks, major obstacles, and major problems. Party officials must have a strong sense of responsibility. They must have both broad shoulders to assume responsibilities and real capability to accomplish goals. They must be both bold in and adept at taking a correct political stance. They must be both resolute in and good at promoting development. They must be both brave in and skilled at advancing reforms. They must be brave enough to squarely face problems and properly resolve them. They must have both the will and the ability to achieve things."

To modernize its governance capacity in the new era, the CPC must do the following:

First, the Party should exercise good political leadership. It should adopt a strategic perspective, and develop creative thinking and a dialectical approach to thinking. It should think in terms of the rule of law, and prepare for the worst-case scenario. It should formulate sound Party lines, principles and policies and resolutely implement them, ensuring that the Party exercises overall leadership and coordinates work in all areas. It should be a good reformer and pioneer. It should be enterprising, work creatively in the light of actual conditions, and adeptly apply information technology, including the Internet, in its work.

Second, the Party should promote sound development. It should effectively put into practice the new development philosophy, and continue to break new ground in development. It should exercise proper law-based governance. It will act more quickly to put in place a system of Party rules and regulations that covers all aspects of Party leadership and Party building, and strengthen and improve Party leadership over bodies of state power.

Third, the Party should engage properly with the people. It will develop new systems, mechanisms, ways and means for this work. It will urge trade unions, Communist Youth League organizations, women's federations, and other people's organizations to strengthen their political consciousness, become more advanced, and better represent the people, to play their role as bridges linking the Party and the people, and to organize and motivate the people to follow the Party.

Fourth, the Party should implement policies soundly. It should be open and frank, take effective measures to address real issues, and seek good outcomes. It should be ready both to act resolutely and swiftly and to make sustained efforts to tackle tough issues head-on. It should have the perseverance to hammer away until a task is done, and make concrete, meticulous and effective efforts in all its work.

Fifth, the Party should manage risk well. It will improve risk prevention and control mechanisms in all areas, skillfully handle various complex issues, overcome all difficulties and obstacles that it meets on its way, and keep a firm hold on the initiative in its work.

To improve the CPC's governance capacity is a long-term, all-encompassing endeavor of vital importance. In its long-term governance, the Party must strive to improve its leadership and governing capabilities, and become more competent, democratic, law-based and modern, so as to seek happiness for the Chinese people, rejuvenation for the Chinese nation, and peace and development for humanity.

图书在版编目（CIP）数据

走向 2049 年的中国 : 英文 / 田应奎等著 ; 外文出
版社英文编译部译 . — 北京 : 外文出版社，2020.6
ISBN 978-7-119-11803-1

Ⅰ . ①走… Ⅱ . ①田… ②外… Ⅲ . ①发展战略—研
究—中国—英文 Ⅳ . ① D60

中国版本图书馆 CIP 数据核字 (2020) 第 116721 号

撰　　稿：田应奎　田　宇　李伟艺
英文翻译：严　晶　闫传海　曹思澄
英文审定：David Ferguson　姜晓宁
责任编辑：蔡莉莉
封面设计：柏拉图创意机构
印刷监制：章云天

走向 2049 年的中国

田应奎　等著

© 2020 外文出版社有限责任公司
出 版 人：徐　步
出版发行：
　　外文出版社有限责任公司（中国北京西城区百万庄大街 24 号　100037）
　　http://www.flp.com.cn
　　电　　话：008610-68320579（总编室）
　　　　　　　008610-68996167（编辑部）
　　　　　　　008610-68995852（发行部）
制　　版：北京杰瑞腾达科技发展有限公司
印　　刷：鸿博昊天科技有限公司
开　　本：787mm×1092mm　1/16
印　　张：14.5
2020 年 10 月第 1 版第 1 次印刷
（英）
ISBN 978-7-119-11803-1
（平）
09600